D1612190

Early Taverns

and

Stagecoach Days in New Jersey

Author's conception of Lyon's ordinary, first tavern in New Jersey, in Newark in 1668.

Early Taverns
and Stagecoach Days
in New Jersey

Walter H. Van Hoesen

Rutherford • Madison • Teaneck
Fairleigh Dickinson University Press
London: Associated University Presses

©1976 by Associated University Presses, Inc.

Associated University Presses, Inc.
Cranbury, New Jersey 08512

Associated University Presses
108 New Bond Street
London W1Y OQX, England

Library of Congress Cataloging in Publication Data

Van Hoesen, Walter Hamilton, 1897—
   Early taverns and stagecoach days in New Jersey.

   Bibliography: p.
   Includes index.
   1. Hotels, taverns, etc.—New Jersey—History. 2. Coach-
ing—New Jersey—History. 3. New Jersey—History—Colonial period, ca. 1600-1775. 4. New Jersey—History—Revolution, 1775-1783. I. Title.
TX909.V36   917.49'04'2   74-198
ISBN 0-8386-1535-X

Other books
by
Walter Hamilton Van Hoesen:

Crafts and Craftsmen of New Jersey

PRINTED IN THE UNITED STATES OF AMERICA

To My Host of Friends who have contributed so much in the way of information and encouragement in support of this project

Contents

Preface   9

1 The First Ordinary   15
2 Public Houses of the Colonial Era in North Jersey   28
3 More of the Colonial Era in North Jersey   49
4 Colonial Taverns in South Jersey   72
5 Inns and Houses during the Revolution and After   97
6 Tavern Customs and Menus   144
7 Stagecoaches and Post Roads   154
8 Wayside Signs and Symbols   168

Bibliography   175
Index   178

Preface

There has long been a need for a historical account of the old taverns and other public houses, as well as the first highways and stagecoach routes, in New Jersey from colonial times until on into the twentieth century. The story was told years ago with respect to New England, Virginia, and other parts of the United States having a past no more interesting or influential than New Jersey's in its impact on this nation's development.

At the outset, when the Dutch first settled Niew Amsterdam on Manhattan Island on the opposite side of the Hudson River early in the 1600s, New Jersey was regarded as part of a vast wilderness they called New Netherland. It stretched from Cape May of the present day on the south to a place on the Connecticut River near Hartford on the north, and west to the banks of the Delaware River. Aside from a few boweries and the tiny settlement called Bergen (Jersey City), the entire country remained virgin.

There was an Indian trail, long known as Raritan Road, leading overland to the Delaware and settlements to the south, and there was also the old Mine Road, laid out by the early Dutch, from Kingston-on-the-Hudson to the mines at Pahaquarry. It crossed the northern part of the present Sussex County. Otherwise the land was unspoiled when the British first took over in the fall of 1664.

In 1687 the state as it now exists was divided by the English into East Jersey and West Jersey. The Province of East Jersey was influenced by the manners and customs of the Dutch and of the Scotch Presbyterians from England, via Long Island and the Connecticut River. In West Jersey, life was dominated by the Quakers, also from England. The two provinces were separated by an invisible line starting on the banks of the Delaware River near Port Jervis in northern New Jersey and taking a southerly course to just east of Leeds Point on the end of Little Egg Harbor Island, on the Atlantic Ocean.

Originally East and West Jersey were simply provinces, with various settlements therein. Then, in 1682, the East Jersey General Assembly, meeting in Elizabethtown, created the four counties of Bergen, Essex, Middlesex, and Monmouth. The counties in West Jersey were apportioned according to boundaries set in 1694 by the West Jersey Assembly meeting in Burlington City; these were Burlington, Cape May (first organized in 1692), Gloucester (first created in 1686), and Salem (settled before 1642).

All of the present counties (there are now twenty-one) were taken from one or more of the original ones. The last to be so set aside was Union, which was taken from Essex in 1856. Oddly enough, it has Elizabeth (Elizabethtown) within its borders, as county seat. The oldest city in the state, it was founded in 1664; Newark, in Essex, was founded in 1666. The founding of Elizabeth 300 years earlier prompted New Jersey's tricentennial celebration of 1964.

In 1784, according to minutes of the State Legislature now on file in Trenton, there were 446 places of public entertainment at that time in New Jersey. They were about evenly divided between East and West Jersey, which had ceased to exist in 1703 when the first royal governor of New York and New Jersey came into office. Royal governors continued until 1738 before New Jersey had its separate appointed governor. That went on until 1776 (the American Revolution broke out in 1775), with William Franklin, son of Benjamin Franklin, as the last royal governor appointed by the king of England. The first governor of the state elected by the Legislature was William Livingston, who served from 1776 until his death in 1790.

Undoubtedly some early taverns have been omited from my list, compiled mostly from license applications, old deeds, and a few diaries. The excuse lies in the times in which we live, and the difficulty of finding original sites.

Within my memory an estimated 200 old structures, many of them taverns dating from the nineteenth century and earlier, have been demolished, abandoned, or just allowed to fall down. Even as these lines are written, plans are underway to remove several outstanding structures. In my travels around the state, I have noted the housing developments and many other changes taking place in the name of progress, and I am surprised that the decline has not been even more severe.

It must be remembered, too, that newspapers and files, at least from the colonial period, are very few. Seldom did tavern or innkeepers keep diaries. Even if they were so disposed, fewer still could even write. This is why I have placed such reliance on license applications. Old court records are silent in many respects. Letters and other memorabilia left behind are far from numerous.

Listing the old taverns and other early public houses in New Jersey has presented a real problem in a number of ways. It was obvious that there were too many for a separate account of each one. Then, too, the state went along for years as separate colonies or settlements within the provinces of East and West Jersey until the first royal governor, and unification did not come until tempers were cooled after the American Revolution.

As the best means of solving the dilemma, I decided to set down accounts of the most widely known and best-remembered establishments according to the early highways. In that way I have also taken into account the later stagecoach routes, days, and customs.

Walter H. Van Hoesen
Fanwood, N. J.

Early Taverns

and

Stagecoach Days in New Jersey

I

The First Ordinary

Diligent research into New Jersey's past reveals the first mention of a hostelry—hostelries were first called ordinaries, then taverns, and finally inns or houses—in *Records of the Town of Newark 1666-1836,* published by the New Jersey Historical Society. The date of first mention was May 16, 1666, soon after the founding of the community on the banks of the Passaic River. The occasion was a meeting of the town's citizenry.

An item of business reads:

> The Town hath chosen the sd. Henry Lyon to keep an Ordinary for the Entertainment of Travellers and Strangers, and desires him to prepare for it as soon as he can.

Thus, true to their New England instinct, neighborliness was always present, second only to Godliness. The establishment of a place where the chance wayfarer might find shelter was next in importance after setting up a meetinghouse for worship. Consideration for the comfort and convenience of the local gentry was a further reason for the desire to establish a common gathering place for the inhabitants.

All traces of that first ordinary, as well as its location, have long since vanished. It was probably made of logs and situated somewhere along Broad Street, which was the first thoroughfare laid out.

Although nothing has been found thus far to prove it, there is little doubt that Elizabethtown, founded in 1664, and the settlements that soon followed at Shrewsbury, Middletown, and Woodbridge, quickly gave serious thought to the need for ordinaries. Great inducements were offered to keep an ordinary, such as setting aside land on which it could be located, pasturage for cattle, and exemption from levies for church and other purposes.

Henry Lyon, the keeper of Newark's first recorded ordinary, was picked by the town fathers for many jobs. Besides being the colony's initial treasurer, he was builder of the first pound where stray cattle were kept, one of three men chosen to oversee erection of fences, and himself an extensive landowner. I recall years ago when the present stop on trolley or jitney busline was called Lyons Farm and not Hillside.

Lyon appears to have opened this ordinary in the closing months of 1668, in response to the directive at town meeting. Few travelers and even fewer strangers patronized it, but he had to provide for bed and board. A bit of liquid refreshment also had to be on hand in the event that local citizens should stop by.

Two years later, in 1670, Lyon transferred the ordinary to Thomas Johnson, another leader in the community, and turned his attention to other matters. Johnson was the colony's tax collector and also the town constable. Besides that, he was keeper of the pound, a carpenter who had worked on the meeting house, and father of the village drummer. By unanimous vote at town meeting, Johnson was given the sole privilege of "selling strong liquors at retail under a gallon, unless in case of necessity, and then by license from a Magistrate."

Jasper Crane, the colony's first magistrate and holder of numerous other offices, was accorded at public meeting in January 1673, the right "to sell liquor." From this it may be assumed that he already maintained or contemplated "a place of public entertainment and shelter," but the records fail to indicate whether he was taking over from Johnson or starting another ordinary on his own.

Action by the town fathers came a few weeks before the first session of the New Jersey Assembly, called by Governor Philip Carteret at Elizabethtown and held from May 26 to 30, 1668. After adopting a harsh criminal code reflecting the Puritan leanings of New England, the delegates directed that the several towns "provide in each instance an ordinary for the Entertainment of Travelers and Strangers as soon as possible."

Consideration for the welfare of travelers and the regulating of the sale of intoxicating beverages seemed sufficiently important to the General Assembly not only to counsel but actually require the opening of some kind of public house in every community. It retained the right to enact legislation pertaining thereto, but in general there was a willingness to leave the power to grant licenses and the details of enforcement up to town meetings and local officials.

The first effort on the part of the English to regulate and control the ordinaries, inns, or taverns in New Jersey was made on April 2, 1664, a matter of weeks after a British naval squadron appeared in New York Bay and took over from the Dutch. Adopted by Governor Nicholls, after King George of England had given to his brother, the Duke of York, all of what is now included within the bounds of New Jersey, the rules are found in "The Duke of York's Laws" and read as follows:

No Person or Persons shall at any time under any pretence or Colour whatsoever undertake to be a Common Victuler, keeper of a

Cookes Shopp or House of Common entertainment, or publique seller of wine, Beare, Ale or strong waters by retail or a less quantity than a quarter Caske, without a Certificate of his good behaviour from the Constable and two Overseers at least of the parish wherein he dwealt and a Lycence first obtained under the hand of two Justices of the peace in the Sessions upon pain of the forfeiting of five pounds for every such offence, or Imprisonment at the discretion of the Court.[1]

In June 1664, the edict became invalid when the Duke of York leased his grant to Berkley and Carteret, but it continued to be the law of the land, so to speak, until 1771. In that year Governor Lovelace of New York, who also exercised authority over New Jersey, and his council, adopted a new rule for certain parts of the land bordering on the Delaware River. It provided:

That the number of Victuallers or Tappers of strong drink be ascertained, that is to say three only for the town (New Castle) and some few up the river, who the officers shall think fit to approve of, and no more than will be found convenient; who may have license to do the same, whereby disorders will be prevented and travellers have better accommodations.[2]

At the meeting of the East Jersey general assembly in May 1668, it was further ordered that "in consideration of the inconveniences that do arise for want of an Ordinary in every town within this province, every town shall provide an Ordinary." Teeth were put in the edict by providing a fine of forty shillings for every month a town went without an ordinary, the fine to go to the county within which the town was located.

1. Charter of William Penn (1879), p. 30.
2. Ibid., p. 448.

The assembly of West Jersey left such matters at first in the hands of the county court concerned, and later up to designated towns. In both East and West Jersey it was contrary to existing rules for any but the holders of licenses to charge for giving lodging or meals to strangers. The rule was particularly obnoxious to people in West Jersey, who frequently lived far removed from the beaten paths and now and then were called upon to give shelter to strangers.

The first ordinaries, according to *A Journal of a Voyage to New York and a Tour in Several of the American Colonies*, written soon after two Labadist missionaries had visited New Jersey in 1679-80, were small indeed. In the northern counties they were made of either logs or stone, while further to the south, boards or brick were used. In either case, the kind and amount of material available were the controlling factor.

An ordinary usually consisted of two small rooms, one with a bar for drinking and for meals, according to Dankert and Sluyter, the two Labadist missionaries. The second room was customarily reserved for the landlord and his family. Travelers had to bed down on the floor of the bar and dining room. Often a lean-to, or shelter, was erected at the rear of the structure for use as a kitchen and woodshed.

As living conditions improved, the eighteenth- and even nineteenth-century taverns, inns, houses, and hotels were more elaborately constructed. I have found, however, that over all the years the custom has continued of keeping the public and so-called family entrances separate. That led, in the early years, to having two doors on the ground floor, with a connecting porch. Often the porch would be divided by a railing or other barrier, so that the landlord's wife and children might sit out to rock and take the air without interfering with, or being bothered by, itinerant travelers and local hangers-on.

It was not long before the ordinary was outmoded, soon to

be replaced by the inn or tavern. I have been asked many times, and often I have questioned native folk, about the difference between an inn and tavern. Invariably the explanation has been the same as what I have heard in England and on the Continent. An inn is an establishment with rooms, catering to overnight travelers, I have been told, while a tavern is a place offering only drinks at a bar, with fun and conviviality. The explanation sounds logical.

I recall very well one of the late-eighteenth-century establishments that has lately joined the ranks of buildings altered beyond recognition. I knew it as a boy as a two-and-a-half-story wooden-framed structure with a porch that entirely encircled its main floor, which was slightly set up from the street. Seven or eight wide steps led up to the barroom, which took up most of the ground floor. At the far end of the porch a second, smaller door led to some steps up to the living quarters on the second floor. To the rear of the dimly lit barroom were several doorways leading to small rooms furnished only with a round table and several chairs. They were reserved for ladies who wished to have drink unseen, and for steady customers who enjoyed a card game while they were drinking. A dining room that opened off the barroom took up the rest of the first floor, except for the kitchen that occupied an extension in the rear.

Upstairs, a single ballroom took up the same space as the barroom on the ground floor. Occasional meetings of fraternal and patriotic groups were held there, and it was otherwise the scene of dances on Friday and Saturday nights. The rest of the second floor was taken up by bedrooms; stairs led to the garret and several other bedrooms usually reserved for the bartender, cook, and waiter.

The records of legislation on a statewide basis and of municipal administration show a vastly changing trend all through New Jersey's history, now in excess of 300 years, shifting from outright prohibition to local option. Laws and regulations have been rigid enough, but enforcement has been another matter. The trend has ranged from severity on the one hand, to utter disregard of either public feelings or welfare on the other.

In view of the problems faced, it is little wonder that keepers of public houses were hard to find in the later part of the 1600s and through most of the 1700s. After the American Revolution, 1775-1783, there was a temporary boost in morale. Every veteran, it seemed, went in for keeping inns, taverns, and houses, largely named after George Washington, the wartime commander-in-chief.

There were many restrictions on the entertainment of strangers. Landlords were required to give the names of all such persons to local magistrates. and the sports of the inn yard, as they came to be known, were frowned upon by the magistrates. All through New Jersey history, both as a colony and state, laws were passed forbidding gamecock fighting, and the records tell of constant raids by constables and sheriff deputies on such gatherings. At the start, such pastimes as "carding, dicing, tally, bowls, billiards, shuffleboard, quoits and ninepins" were taboo. Eventually shuffleboard, bowls, quoits, and ninepins were permitted under local option.

Even into the early years of the twentieth century, the efforts to prevent fights between gamecocks continued. When I was a small boy, I recall, such encounters were held stealthily in the barnyards of several inns in the country town of Scotch Plains, where I grew up. Boys were not allowed, but many of the men in the village assembled in a circle lit only by the faint glow of an oil lantern and the stars, while two fighting roosters battled it out in the center space.

The birds were carefully raised and brought to the fight by their owners. Money was wagered on the outcome and each fighting cock had its cheering section. News of a particularly strong fighter was spread by word of mouth, and on occasion the champion from another town in the county was brought in. Too often the unusual activity and muffled cheering were sufficient to bring the village marshal to investigate. But by the time he appeared, the crowd, contestants, and money were likely to have evaporated into the night.

Drunkards were never accepted at inns, although many a time men who had imbibed to excess were escorted home or to a place in the hayloft to "sleep it off." Penalties were imposed on innkeepers and tavern owners tippling in their establishments, and men who appeared in court charged with ignoring warnings to leave such premises were dealt with harshly by the magistrates.

All through the colonial period there were few occasions of public intoxication. By the time the American Revolution had arrived and the 1800s were embarked on, every town and hamlet in the state had its local "characters" who imbibed too much, were considered unreliable, and were deemed useful only for odd jobs.

"Jersey Lightning" was really over-aged apple cider, an evil concoction known even late in the 1600s. Its exact origin is lost in history, but the early records reveal that it was taboo with the Indians, who gave it the name of "firewater" and really went mad when they drank too much of it. Records also indicate that even the pioneer settlers knew the potent quality of fermented apple cider.

It was illegal to serve "Jersey Lightning" in the first ordinaries, and even later when they were called taverns, inns, and houses. On occasion, however, it came in handy as a substitute for whiskey or wines imported from Great Britain and other foreign lands. It was certainly just as strong, especially when made from Jersey apples.

"Jersey Lightning" was nothing more than hard cider. Now and then it was fermented and even refermented when people were not content with the natural aging process. A favorite testing method was to hold a drop or two between thumb and forefinger to see if it strung out when the digits were held a few inches apart. That was the way farmers tested their product, and drinkers standing at the bar long held the notion that it was the only way to determine that they were getting the genuine article and not a substitute.

I recall an incident very early in the present century when, as a small boy, I had gained entry unseen into a local barroom. A village character had become noisily drunk, and to shut him up the men at the bar hustled him through a rear door into the enclosed courtyard. His continued protestations led his abductors literally to bury him in a nearby manure pile. Once back in the barroom, they began to worry whether the drunk would suffocate in the event that he did not get free. They went back and, while the rest looked on, one of the men took a long-handled pitchfork that was leaning against the barn and prodded the manure pile, hoping to find the victim of their horseplay. As long as the drunk lived, he was always identifiable by the one good eye he had left. Occasionally, after much urging, he would also show scars on his body made by the pitchfork jabs.

On another occasion an entirely different character (there were several in the village) tried to invade the elementary school I was attending, after he had imbibed too freely of "Jersey Lightning." The principal, Mr. Hendrickson, calmly led the man to the front gate by the back of his shabby collar, and in front of a gaping crowd of schoolchildren then planted his right foot on the seat of his pants and sent him sprawling into the gutter.

Neither the Dutch nor the Swedes, groups of whom had settled in parts of New Jersey prior to the English, appear to have set up hostelries where occasional travelers could find shelter. The Dutch had boweries, or farms, in the Communipaw area, along present-day New York Bay, soon after settling on Manhattan Island across the Hudson River. They even founded the village of Bergen (Jersey City) in 1630.

In 1642-43 the Swedes settled at the mouth of the Salem River in South Jersey and founded Fort Elfsborg. It was abandoned soon afterwards because of an overabundance of mosquitoes. In 1655 Peter Stuyvesant led an army of 155 men to wrest control of the area from the Swedes for the Dutch East India Company. He returned to New Amsterdam in triumph, but subsequent efforts at colonization did not include any ordinaries, inns, or taverns.

The keepers of ordinaries, taverns, or inns and houses were among the most knowledgeable and influential men during the colonial era, the American Revolutionary period, and on into the 1800s. Whatever public life there was found expression in their establishments.

It was in the first ordinaries that town meetings were held. Later, boards of freeholders and community councils met in the same places, until town halls and other buildings of sufficient size became available. The proprietors of public houses were the first to learn of action taken or pending in the legislature, whether on a state level, in the county, or locally.

The innkeeper or taverner was an intimate of lawyers. He knew that a decision on an important issue of law could be made only after drinks had been passed back and forth. To him was referred for settlement any dispute over cards, the price of lottery tickets, or the sale of cattle. He was expected to have the latest information regarding the health of the governor or any other notable person, whether or not he was known to be ill. Bills of sale and sheriff foreclosures were also matters supposed to be within his knowledge. The inn or travern keeper was also supposed to be a good judge of human nature, to keep an eye open for runaway slaves, to watch out for errant travelers who had a bad habit of departing without payment of charges, and to pay respectful attention to ladies on the occasions when they were forced to "take to the open road." In most cases the landlord, as he was often called, was prohibited by local ordinance, backed up by state legislation, from "knowingly harbouring in house, barn or stable any rogues, vagabonds, thieves, beggers or masterless men or women."[3] Our ancestors were God-fearing people, and they reacted kindly to strangers in their midst, but it was an entirely different matter when it came to heedless or recalcitrant persons.

In some communities landlords were not permitted to sell "sack or strong waters," or to allow dancing or singing on their premises. The prices of wine and beer, and of meals, were regulated in most instances, almost from the start. In 1693 the town fathers of Burlington, according to the minutes for a meeting on March 12 of that year, set the price of a meal at "six pence and not above a penny for an ale-quart of Beare (beer) out of mealtime."

It would seem strange to one steeped in antiques, as I have been, not to make mention of the furnishings in New Jersey's early public houses. Not that there are any remaining—there are none—but it is nice to know that thought was given to such things.

The furnishings of the very first ordinaries are not known, of course, and even the sites of the buildings are for the most part unknown. In the northern part of the state the old ordinaries for the most part succumbed to "progress," and their furnishings are in the same category. In the southern counties a few of the old public houses from the middle 1700s survived in various states of decrepitude, but here again their furnishings are gone.

---

3. **Ordinances of Newark (1801).**

By the time of the Revolution, however, there were a number of public sales, and these establish that the furnishings of public houses of that time were plentiful. Some of these establishments survive to this day, but their bedsteads, bureaus, and other furniture are not claimed to be of equal age. Not until we come to the Civil War era and later do we find interesting memorabilia. Only pieces of crockery and glassware in use before the Revolution remain on special view.

I have a Windsor rocker said to have been used in the Stage House Inn at Scotch Plains by Recompense Stanbury when he owned the establishment soon after the Revolution. The chair had been removed to the Stanbury house, which then stood at the intersection of Park Avenue and the road to Springfield. It was bought early in this century at an auction of the Stanbury household goods by my grandfather, who attended the sale holding me, then a small boy, by the hand. Obviously made as a standing Windsor, the chair has nine instead of the usual seven reeds in the rounded back. Originally of mahogany, its rockers are of maple or birch and were added sometime after the invention of rocking chairs, in 1747, ascribed to the many-sided genius of Benjamin Franklin.

The maker of the chair and its further history are not known. It is undoubtedly the oldest piece of furniture in the entire Scotch Plains area, and is a rare example of tavern furniture, although many other old pieces may be kept today in private hands. The descendants of onetime inkeepers in Burlington, Bordentown, Mt. Holly, and other areas in South Jersey are reputed to have some of the furnishings from such public houses, but I have found these people reluctant to discuss what they do or do not have.

The Windsor rocker is now on loan by me to the Scotch Plains-Fanwood Historical Society and is on exhibition in its headquarters, the Cannonball House, directly across from the Stage House Inn, which is now operated as a restaurant.

Stage House Inn in Scotch Plains, dating from 1737. Now a restaurant.
PHOTOGRAPHED IN 1973, COURTESY RICHARD M. LEA.

Stage House Inn in Scotch Plains as it was in 1890. Built by Sutton in
1737, it was referred to on Erskin's map as Marsella's Tavern. This
photograph shows the original Liberty Pole where a monument now
stands.

2

Public Houses of the Colonial Era in North Jersey

The descriptive word *Ordinary* had pretty much disappeared from use and had been replaced by *Inn* or *Tavern* when the comparatively few such establishments in New Jersey entered the 1700s. They were restricted mostly to the firmly established settlements, and another quarter-century had to pass before a demand arose for such places along the open road.

With the stagecoach routes between New York and Philadelphia and other places in between, there arose a real need for inns or taverns. They were placed at strategic spots along the Old Mine Road as it crossed the northern part of the state, along the Old York Road, along the King's Highway, more popularly known as St. George Avenue, and elsewhere along the stagecoach lanes that grew as the traveling public gained in number.

The need for inns, of course, exceeded that for taverns. There had to be rooms to accommodate the weary travelers and provision for changing horses, and the latter need led to the erection of stables to shelter both fresh and spent ani-

8

mals. Hay and grain had to be provided and men engaged as grooms, stable boys, and just for doing odd jobs.

Until the American Revolution started in 1775 and the century was three-quarters spent, the state continued as really two separate entities—East and West Jersey. There were separate assemblies and governments. East Jersey was under the jurisdiction of the royal governor in New York, while West Jersey was controlled by William Penn and his Quaker friends in neighboring Pennsylvania. Records of inns and taverns from those times clearly show the line of demarcation—East Jersey with four counties and West Jersey with the same number.

Any discussion of the inns and taverns of New Jersey's colonial period must start with the Old Mine Road. In the first place, it was undoubtedly the first highway in the country, dating from the mid-1600s. Second, it has largely fallen into bad times and its original route is not easy to find.

Pahaquarry

I shall have a great deal more to say about the Old Mine Road later on. Suffice it to say for the moment that I have spent many pleasant hours, and even days, tracing its neglected course, starting at Kingston (Esopus)-on-the-Hudson and ending at Pahaquarry on the Delaware, after crossing the northern part of still-rural Sussex county. I have talked with natives and explored old ruins without finding a trace of the colonial public houses.

There certainly must have been inns or taverns in those long-ago times. Only those of more recent origin, in most instances dating no further back than the turn of the present century, are with us today, doing an uncertain business. I had to depend solely on musty records and local history or tradition to find any traces at all.

Walpack

Beginning at a point where the ancient road crossed over the border from New York State to New Jersey and going westward, I discovered in Walpack Township the stone building that had been erected about 1750 by Isaac Van Campen as an inn and lodging place for occasional weary travelers who chanced by. Local history records that it sheltered such prominent figures as John Adams, when he had occasion to journey to and from his native Massachusetts to attend sessions of the Continental Congress in Philadelphia. Later, according to tradition, he stopped there when he was President and then a member of Congress.

General Horation Gates and General Casimir Pulaski, two Revolutionary patriots, are said to have made the inn their headquarters while troops were camped nearby during fighting in the area. Because of its historical importance, the U. S. Department of the Interior plans to relocate the structure on higher ground when the meadow where it stands is flooded by the Tock Island development.

According to the late C. G. Hine, who in 1908 wrote a book on the Old Mine Road after wandering over its entire length, an iron fireback made for the inn by the Oxford Furnace in neighboring Warren County was dated 1742 when he saw it. Owner Van Campen later became a member of the state's Legislature, from 1782 to 1785. About 1811 a son, Abraham Van Campen, sold the property to a Henry DeWitt of Rochester, New York, for his son, John H. DeWitt, and it ceased to be an inn.

Mine Brook

About halfway between Walpack Bend and the Delaware Water Gap, on the Mine Brook, is the site of Henry Shoemaker's old Union Hotel. Many years ago it was located for me by the late B. B. Edsall, who had a reputation as "the best-informed historian in the county of Sussex."

Shoemaker is recorded in Sussex history as being "a soldier of the Revolution." Just when he operated the Union Hotel is unknown, but it is a matter of local tradition that the building was erected prior to the Revolution. Shoemaker did most of his fighting in the general vicinity of Walpack, history records, and one of his encounters was with a Tory by the name of Barton. The story is still told by oldtimers in Sussex.

After the fighting ceased, so the story goes, Shoemaker turned his living abode into a hotel. Friends and neighbors spent many rollicking evenings there, as did the occasional travelers who were sheltered for the night. He is said even to have maintained fresh horses for stages on the way from Kingston to Philadelphia and further south and for those northbound from such places.

The Union Hotel never operated as such after the death of Shoemaker in the early 1800s. The general decline of business, coupled with the fact that he left no family, and the coming of the railroad a few years later, were sufficient to bring about the early demise of the venture. According to natives in the area, the structure has not been standing for nearly a century.

Montague and Brick House

Next we come to Montague and its Brick House, with the latter name well enough known to appear frequently on maps and even signposts. Brick House, the record shows, was built in 1776 by Roger Clark, who is said to have used bricks that were fired within three-quarters of a mile of the spot. Almost from the start Brick House was a famed stopping place, and for years the stage from Oswego to New York included it as a regular point of call.

It is one of those bits of local history that Judge James Stoll, at the time a Philadelphian, had tried for many years to get possession of Brick House, but he and Clark could never come to terms. Judge Stoll at last got a liquor dealer, a fellow-Philadelphian, to purchase the inn and then turn it over to him. The Judge had a summer home on an adjoining property and he even arranged, in like manner, to have the sale include land for a garden.

Judge Stoll is recorded as owner for years, but he never ran the place as an inn. Instead, he rented to various persons in whose names licenses were issued. They sold strong drink to everybody and catered to the traveling public. For years it was a stopping place for the stage line that ran from Deckertown to Jersey City.

Operations continued almost without interruption until the mid-1950s. Brick House was finally, and permanently, removed a few years ago to make room for a traffic circle opening to another crossing of the Delaware to Milford, Pennsylvania. In the course of demolition, the wreckers are reported to have found a secret closet holding several flintlock muskets of Revolutionary vintage.

Flatbrookville

On the way through Flatbrookville enroute to Pahaquarry, I stopped at the Flatbrook Hotel, but it was of comparatively recent origin, dating only from the 1890s. Pahaquarry is disappointing, really not much more than a big hill. There are only two settlements in all of Pahaquarry Township, and Millbrook, which is one of them, is said to date from 1839, when Conrad Welter erected the first stone house. It was known for years as the "Methodist Tavern," and Welter is known to have sheltered many early circuit riders of the faith who came to the area to address home meetings.

But Welter did not run a general hostelry open to all. As a matter of fact, I traveled over almost all of Sussex without finding further trace of colonial inns or taverns, except for those in the few towns along the way. True, there are establishments that cater to the motoring public in such places as the town of Sussex, just over the border from New York State, Port Jervis on the Jersey side, Newton, Hope, and so on. Some of them claim old origins, but none dates before the founding of the respective communities, which in almost every instance was in the early 1800s.

By the time the Revolution started, various sections of the Old Mine Road had fallen into disrepair or disuse because of short-cuts, as a more usable colonial road was laid out. I shall have more to say about this in a later chapter. Suffice it to say that a little east of Hope it had been joined by a colonial stage road that started at Hackensack, in Bergen County, and traversed Passaic, Horseneck, Morristown, Mendham, Chester, and Hackettstown. There were inns in each of these places where horses could be changed and weary passengers might find food and shelter.

Hackensack

In Hackensack there is the Peter Zabriskie House, still standing after more than 200 years. It was erected in 1751 and used as headquarters by George Washington in August 1776, when the Continental troops were encamped along the Jersey side of the Hudson. It was operated for many years as an inn for travelers and a tavern for local gentry. Stagecoaches started at Zabriskie's and went westward to Philadelphia and points south.

In the 1800s it was operated successively as a bank, post

office, and restaurant, all using the first floor of the three-story structure. Upstairs the rooms were maintained for occasional travelers brought in by the railroad after stage-coaches became a thing of the past. Fronting on the main square of the town, it has twenty-three rooms, and when I was last there, room 19 on the second floor was pointed out to me as Washington's. The only distinguishing mark about the Zabriskie House is a bronze plaque set into the side of the building by the Bergen County Historical Society.

Passaic and Horseneck

At Passaic and Horseneck there were colonial inns, but of details of ownership and dates, even natives in the area are lacking in knowledge. General Robert Erskine, who became Washington's first surveyor general, lists both places in his maps of the region, but he fails to note by whom the inns were run during either the Revolutionary or colonial periods, according to the late Albert H. Heusser, Paterson newspaperman, in *The Forgotten General*. The two towns were points of exit for the iron ore mined at the Ringwood mines under supervision of Erskine, and it is highly probable that they had a demand for inns.

Morristown

The Arnold Tavern, which stood on the north side of the village square in Morristown, is said to have been built about 1740 by a Samuel Arnold. The historian Sir George Trevelyan notes that it was the headquarters for General Washington "between the seventh of January and the twenty-eighth of May, 1777." Every single one of Washington's dispatches during that period is dated from Morristown.

Old Arnold Tavern at Morristown, dating from about 1740. Now demolished, it was Washington's headquarters in 1777. COURTESY THE NEW JERSEY HISTORICAL SOCIETY.

Before the Revolution, the Arnold Tavern was kept by a Thomas Kinney, high sheriff of Morris County and a large landowner. The property at that time included a farm that extended in the rear back to Jocky Hollow Road. Colonel Jacob Arnold, son of the first proprietor, was an aide on Washington's staff and paymaster for the Continental Army, which was quartered in Jocky Hollow.

Writing at a later date on his "Travels in North America," the Marquis de Chastellux, who made a trip through New Jersey in 1780, had this to say about the Arnold Tavern:

I intended stopping in Morristown only to bait my horses, for it was only half past two, but on entering the inn of Mr Arnold, I saw a dining room adorned with looking glasses and handsome mahogany furniture and a table spread for twelve persons. I learned that all the preparation was for me, and what affected me more nearly was to see a dinner that corresponded with appearances ready to serve up. I was indebted for this to General Washington and the precaution of Colonel O'Mayland, who was sent before to acquaint them of my arrival. It would have been very ungracious of me to have accepted this dinner at the expense of Mr. Arnold, who is an honest man and not a particle in common with Benedict Arnold. It would have been still more awkward to have paid for the banquet without eating it. I therefore instantly determined to dine in the comfortable inn.

There were other inns, or taverns, in Morristown during the Revolutionary period; they will be dealt with later.

Mendham and Basking Ridge

In Mendham the Blackhorse Tavern is still standing on the main street, after more than 200 years. It was built in 1743 by Ebenezer Byram, who had come from Bridgewater, in Massachusetts. He is credited also with changing the name of the hamlet from Roxiticus and building the ancient Presbyterian Church at its present location on the crest of a hill, which is to the right as the traveler approaches Mendham from Basking Ridge.

The Blackhorse Tavern was known for miles as a famed stop on the old stagecoach line to and from Hackensack, and even to and from points across the Hudson and in New England. Tired horses were changed for fresh ones, and the hulking figure of Byram was always to be seen, out to greet each stage arrival and see to the comfort of its passengers.

The graves of Ebenezer and numerous other Byrams lie in the old cemetery adjacent to the church. He is said to have operated the tavern for more than forty years and, at one time or another, to have held every public office in Mendham.

The story is told by natives in Mendham about the village character who entered the Blackhorse Tavern one night, shouting and making a nuisance of himself. According to Robert V. Hoffman, in his book *The Revolutionary Scene in New Jersey,* "the landlord promptly abated the roustabout by knocking him down with a dinner pail." Hoffman adds that the Blackhorse Tavern is one of the few pre-Revolutionary hostelries in the entire state that is still standing.

Chester and Hackettstown

There was also a hotel on the main street of Chester, which in pre-Revolutionary days was known as Black River after the stream that ran nearby. At Hackettstown, shortly before the road joined with the main line from Sussex to Phillipsburg, was still another. The two catered to the weary traveler as well as local gentry and both continue in business today, although on a different basis.

Oxford

Again on the main line, before reaching Phillipsburg, was the hamlet of Oxford, known in colonial times only for the famed Oxford Furnace. It had a tavern that catered to the needs of some fifty workers at one time employed at the furnace. Stages did not have this tavern as a regular stop and any record of the various keepers has been lost. The tavern has long since disappeared and even its site is unknown.

South Orange

The onetime South Orange Hotel, reputedly "the oldest structure in town" and said to date from the early 1700s, survived until April 1969, when it was torn down as a public hazard. Condemned as unsafe and occupied for years only by a small repair shop on the ground floor, it stood at South Orange Avenue and Valley Street.

Village records go back only to 1869, but local tradition says that the original part of the structure was erected in 1700 on land owned by John Treat, son of Robert Treat, a founder of Newark in 1666. Samuel Thompkins bought the inn and the land on which it stood in 1714. He and his descendants operated the inn until 1804, and for more than a century it was a stopping place for travelers and stagecoaches bound to and from Newark or New York.

In 1804 Marcus Ball bought the property, erected an addition, and continued the hotel. Then, about 1900, Ball's descendants sold the property to Jack Hart. He converted the building into apartments upstairs, with several shops on the ground floor. During the prohibition era in the late 1920s it was bought by P. J. Smith, the village blacksmith, who operated the tavern for a short time. In 1960 it was sold again, this time to the Bellin family, owners of a local dry goods store. Mrs. Etta Bellin was the last proprietor.

Aside from the small repair shop on the ground floor, the building had not been used for years. The bedrooms upstairs had been empty for a quarter of a century. The stairs leading up to them were rotted, and they creaked loudly. A former service station and tire shop on the ground floor had long since been vacated.

Clinton (Hunt's Mills)

Originally known as Hunt's Mills, this tiny hamlet on the Raritan River was renamed in honor of New York's Governor DeWitt Clinton in 1828 and bears the name Clinton to this day. The Clinton House, founded in 1743, was the community's first major structure, and it still stands unchanged in many respects. During the Revolution the town was nothing

Clinton Inn in Clinton, in 1973. Founded in 1743.

more than a crossroads and a stagecoach stop on the New Brunswick-Easton road.

According to the 1840 edition of Barber and Howes' *Historical Collections,* which contains a "view of Clinton from Quarry Hill," Daniel Hunt and his sons erected several mills and the Clinton House along the South Branch of the Raritan in the eighteenth century. The village clustered about the inn grew, and in 1820, according to the account, contained three dwellings and a tannery, besides the mills and inn owned by the Hunts.

The main road to Easton formerly ran a course through town along the South Branch of the Raritan. In recent years Route 78 has diverted much of the traffic to outside the town. The original Hunt's mills have been restored and are now occupied by the Hunterdon County Art Center and the Clinton Historical Museum. The old inn continues, although its dining room now caters to motorists and seldom are there any demands for shelter. The history of its owners and inn-keepers is not known after the last of the Hunts died in the early 1800s.

At Hunt's Mills there was a tavern in 1764. Abraham Bonnel was there from that year until his death in 1797. It became known far and wide as Bonnel's Tavern, and during the Revolutionary War it was frequented by many prominent people as well as the farmers round about. A company of militia was formed there composed of Hunterdon men, and in 1777 Bonnel was elected Lt. Colonel of the Second Regiment, Hunterdon County Militia. More will be said of Bonnel's Tavern in a succeeding chapter.

Crawford's Corners

Along the old road that in colonial times ran from Pittstown to Morristown, where it intersected another road from Easton to New Brunswick, John Crawford for many years kept a tavern that was built in 1765. In 1785 he advertised it for rent, describing it as "A large commodious house, 3 stories high, with 4 rooms on the Lower Floor and 3 on the second; a large kitchen, and a fireplace in it." Apparently it found no takers, because Crawford later applied to the state Legislature for a license and kept the place until his death in 1815. Adjacent to the house were two stables and a good horse shed.

The Crawford Tavern was for many years a favorite stopping place for stages on both roads until they stopped running for lack of business. Even then it was operated for some years after Crawford's death by his widow and then others as a place patronized by local men.

Captain Thomas Jones kept a tavern near Clinton, in Lebanon Township, as early as 1760. In that year he is recorded in the annals of West Jersey as having applied for a license. He last appears as an applicant in 1788, when he sought a renewal from the state legislature. His activities during the Revolution will be reported in a subsequent chapter.

White House

There was only one tavern in White House during the colonial era. It was built about 1750 by Abraham Van Horn, at the crossing of Rockaway Creek on the road from Clinton to Somerville. It was known as the White House, as was the village that gradually grew up around it. Its location caused it to become a favorite stop for stage lines and travelers alike from Easton, New Brunswick, and other points.

In 1760 Van Horn turned the operation over to his son, Arthur, who kept it until 1775, when he was followed by John Connel, according to license application records. Next came Aaron T. Luckas, who moved there from New Germantown. In 1781, also according to license application records, he was succeeded by Cornelius Tunison, who was also at other locations previously.

The Hickory Tavern "in Bethlehem, to the South Branch of the Raritan," is said to date from 1756. I do not know for whom, or by whom, it was built, but in a report of commissions fixing the boundaries of Hunterdon and Sussex counties dated May 8 of that year and now on file in both county seats, it is mentioned in connection with changes to the road "leading from Hickory Tavern." The road apparently ran between Pittstown and Bloombury.

In 1767 a John Emley leased the site for a period of seven years to John and Adonijah Farnesworth, with the proviso that they "build a good Logg House, at least 28 foot by 22, a good Cellar under the Whole to be Walled with Stones, build a good kitchen, a good barn and Stables, etc. to replace the present structure, which has fallen on Evil Times."

Under the name of Hickory Tavern the place prospered, but the Farnesworths sold their lease to Spencer Carter, who was succeeded by Peter Howell when he became involved in the Revolutionary fighting.

Flemington

The first license issued by the West Jersey authorities in what later became known as Flemington was to Samuel Fleming in 1746. It was a log house fronting on the old road to Howell's Ferry (Stockton). In 1756, ten years later, he erected a new house, according to his license application. It was on the road that ran from what eventually came to be known as Rockafellow's Mills on the Raritan River to Reading's Ferry. His last application was on May 20, 1766. That same year he sold the property to Dr. James Creed, who carried on for two years before selling out to Nathaniel Lowery.

Other Flemington taverns started in the pre-Revolutionary era were one kept by Nathaniel Parker in 1774 and one by John Anderson in 1772.

Retracing our steps a little, we reach the charming town of Chatham, in northern New Jersey, just off the spur stage line of olden times from Hackensack westward. Residents say that the first tavern and inn in the area was built about 1755 by Timothy Day. It stood north of Morris Avenue, they say, near the intersection with River Road leading to Turkey (New Providence).

A second hostelry in Chatham is said to have followed soon afterward, as travel and the demand for shelter grew. Most of the early travel was along Morris Avenue to Springfield, Elizabeth, and Newark to the east, and Morristown toward the west. The names of the various proprietors have been lost with passing time.

Day's Tavern, after being run for years by Timothy, was taken over in 1792 by his son, Israel, according to a History of Chatham published in 1964, the result of a joint effort by hundreds of the community's residents. Various landlords followed until 1860, when clouds of civil war began to gather. Travel along Morris Avenue declined with the coming of the railroad and competition turned the structure, long since demolished, to other uses.

Newark

After Newark's start as site of the state's first tavern on record, it is not surprising to find that there were others there during the colonial period. Two establishments stand out, and after the Revolution they were joined by still others. First, there was the Eagle and second, the Rising Sun. Both were on Broad Street. Few travelers passed by without stopping at one or the other for a glass or two of spirits to fortify them for the further journey.

The Rising Sun was the starting point in 1768 for the eastbound stages operated by the partnership of Matthias Ward and John Thompson, two leading citizens of Newark. By 1772 there were four competing stage lines, all starting from the Eagle Tavern. Both places were filled with strangers stopping by to exchange information picked up at inns from Boston southward to Charlestown. Talk of resistance to

Britain was heard in the taproom and local stalwarts promised support.

Jersey City

History and tradition have combined to preserve the records of two hostelries in the ancient village of Bergen (Jersey City) during the colonial era. In the Free Public Library in Jersey City, there is a cornerstone taken originally from the Peter Stuyvesant Tavern in Manhattan. According to Robert Hoffman, in his interesting book on Revolutionary episodes in New Jersey, the stone was used about 1745 in the foundation of Daddy Tise's Tavern, which stood on Bergen Avenue (the present Glenwood Avenue) until it was demolished in the 1940s. The stone bears the initials *P. S.* on one side. Washington and his aides are said to have stopped there for refreshments in 1775.

The second hostelry in old Bergen of the colonial period was Black Sam's Tavern. Daniel Van Winkle, revered as a local historian until his death in the 1930s, has failed to give its exact location in any of his writings. Nor did Harriet Phillips Eaton give it in her *Jersey City: Its Historic Sites,* published in 1898 and now out of print. However, in a charming little story concerning Janetje Van Ripen Tours, Mrs. Eaton went so far at a later date as to locate the Tours House "at Bergen Avenue and Mercer Street, near Black Sam's Tavern."

According to Mrs. Eaton, the Tours young lady frequently depended on Black Sam for information about the British during the Revolution. Officers and men often gathered at his tavern and gossiped about pending moves. She would pass such information along to General Anthony Wayne near Hackensack. According to the story, the go-between was a brother, Daniel Van Ripen, who daily took food prepared by Mrs. Tours to Americans imprisoned by the British on ships docked in the Hudson.

One day, the Eaton story continues, Mrs. Tours got to Black Sam's tavern so tired she could go no further. Black Sam, standing in the doorway, saw her. Leading her along a hall to a rear room, he succeeded in not attracting the attention of the noisy Britishers in the evil-smelling bar. He closed the door before drawing a chair near the fireplace for her to rest, while he stirred the red hot embers into a flame. Warning her about getting too tired in lugging large parcels of food for the prisoners, he went to the kitchen for a meal to give her strength.

Black Sam told the tired girl of overhearing some British officers talking about a plot to capture West Point. That night Mrs. Tours, so the story goes, repeated to her brother what Black Sam had recited. He started out for Hackensack and informed General Anthony Wayne. In that manner the American forces were able to frustrate Benedict Arnold in his scheme to turn West Point over to the enemy.

Pottersville

Once more turning westward and passing the old towns of Watchung, Liberty Corners, Bedminster, and Peapack-Gladstone, each of which must have had a now-forgotten colonial tavern or inn, we come to Pottersville. It was at different times called Potters Mills and Lamington Falls. The first hostelry was kept by Casper Berger from about 1762 until 1772. In the latter year Berger is known to have moved to Readington. He was a German stonemason who had landed in Philadelphia in 1744, his passage fare paid by Cornelius Van Horn of White House.

Berger, who became influential in that part of Jersey, sold the Pottersville tavern to John Wyckoff, who kept it until 1780, when he moved to nearby New Germantown (Oldwick). Other landlords were Andrew Aumock, Philip Rose, Arthur Hewarie, and, in 1786, Jeremiah Fisher. When I knew the place as a boy it was called Sutton's Hotel, but when it changed, or the owner's full name, I do not know. During the early 1900s and the days of the railroad from White House to Morristown, it enjoyed a brief revival.

Oldwick

There were two colonial taverns at New Germantown, which changed its name to Oldwick when World War I made anything German distasteful. The first one was started by Archer Gifford. He died in 1761 and his widow soon married a John Welsh, who operated it until 1768. It was at Main and Church streets, across from the first Lutheran church to be erected in America, early in the 1700s. In 1772 it was kept by a Godfrey Rhinehart and on June 12, 1777, it was taken over by the Zion Church Corporation. In 1801 it was torn down to be replaced by a new structure.

The second tavern at New Germantown was kept by a Samuel Adams, who was there in 1759. After a brief closing and resumption of operations by a Mrs. Isabel Drake, Adams took over again in 1767. Aaron T. Luckas took over for a time when Adams died, according to an announcement of the time, and in 1789 a Henry Teeple stated that "he has lately rented the noted Stand in New Germantown which for upwards of twenty years past has been occupied as a public House of Entertainment." In 1796 it was kept by a Samuel Heath, who abandoned it to destruction four years later.

Hillsborough

One of the first establishments in what was then, and still is, a mostly rural area was Woods Tavern, in Hillsborough, in Somerset county. It had been a landmark along the old Amwell Road from 1726 until it was finally destroyed by fire in 1932. If a visitor had asked its whereabouts during the days of so-called national prohibition, he would have had no difficulty whatever. Now the site is covered with weeds and residents of the present time do not even know its former location.

The original hostelry was near the present Route 206 running from Somerville to Princeton, and it was known for years as "The Tavern in the Woods." Later it was shortened to Woods Tavern, which still has a habit of cropping up on Somerset county maps.

The tavern property included broad acreage that was fenced to provide overnight accommodations for horses, cattle, sheep wagons, and produce belonging to travelers who put up at the tavern. Huge barns and stables were also available to patrons.

History records that the guest rooms were always filled at the old tavern. The kitchen, the bar, and even the dining room were frequently pressed into use. Now and then there were "exhibitions" of cockfighting, or a traveling musician would saw away on his fiddle for dancing. The stranger was almost immediately put on his mettle, and tests of strength would follow, to the great delight of hangers-on. Natives from the neighborhood and the nearby Sourland Mountains would dance there almost nightly, with occasional vistors from Trenton and other "remote" places.

Business at the tavern began to decline with the end of the

Civil War. Travel on the Amwell Road slackened when two railroads were constructed and reached into every hamlet of southern Somerset and Hunterdon counties. The old place temporarily sprang again into popularity in 1872, when Horace Greeley, editor of the *New York Tribune,* was campaigning for president. On the way from Jersey City to Lambertville, he tarried long enough to speak from the steps of the aging structure. Suffice it to say that he lost the election to General Ulysses S. Grant. The tavern finally bowed to the inevitable and closed its doors for the last time in the late 1800s.

3

More of the Colonial Era in North Jersey

The King's Highway, later called St. George Avenue, was another important thoroughfare in colonial times. It started at Staten Island Sound, went west on present-day Elizabeth Avenue in Elizabethtown, to Broad street, and thence on to Rahway (Bridgetown) and to New Brunswick before crossing the Raritan and proceeding across the state to Trenton. I shall have more to say later of this great route's importance during and long after the Revolution. Let it suffice for the moment to remark that in the colonial era it was a major link to New York, by boat and ferry, with Elizabethtown and points north, and with New Brunswick, Trenton, Philadelphia, and places to the south.

Elizabeth

Originally named in honor of the reigning British king, the road was open its full length prior to the 1700s. The tavern right off the water's edge that greeted thirsty travelers bound west from New York was the first of many along the long road. It was there that the stages started and many a man, according to early history, began his journey in various degrees of sobriety after partaking too generously of refreshment at the tavern bar while awaiting the stage.

It is a pity that all trace of that first tavern has been lost with the passage of time. I have checked the early records of Essex county, in which it was located, for another 180-odd years, also those of Elizabethtown and Trenton, without avail.

The Red Lion Inn, at the corner of Broad Street and Rahway Avenue, a site now occupied by the city's public library, was one of the first in Elizabethtown. It was initially owned by William Williamson and, after his death in 1734, by his widow, Margaret. She married William Chetwood a few years later. In 1764 it was called the Marquis of Granby. When Samuel Smith owned it in 1771, he was the one to name it The Red Lion Inn.

A famous place in its day was the Union Hotel, which stood on South Broad Street, Elizabethtown, from 1757 until it was destroyed by fire on January 10, 1867. Built originally by Mathias Williamson, it quickly became a gathering place for residents of the colonial town and a place where travelers were sure of a hearty welcome.

As early as 1728 a long, low, one-and-a-half-story structure used as a tavern stood in South Broad Street, Elizabethtown, near the bridge over the Elizabeth River. In that year it was conveyed "by John Morris, yeoman, to John Dennis, innholder." The latter sold the property to Edward Thomas in 1730, after less than two years' ownership. Thomas operated the place as a tavern for the next thirty years until death intervened and it was inherited by a son, who took it through the Revolutionary period and beyond.

A grandson of Edward Thomas by the name of Robinson Thomas was next to inherit the property, and about 1795 he erected the famed Carteret Arms on the site. Operated at first as a hostelry, it was then occupied by the Elizabeth Orphan Asylum and, much later, by the Elizabeth Public Library until 1913, when the library moved almost directly across the street to a building especially erected for it at the site of the old Red Lion Inn. Also in 1913, the Carteret Arms was purchased by the Elizabeth Historic and Civic Association and remodeled as a center for historic, patriotic, and women's organizations.

Another early landmark in Elizabethtown was long known as Graham's Tavern at the northwest corner of Broad and West Jersey Streets. One of the city's largest department stores now occupies the site. Erected in the 1760s, it was a leading meeting place for patriotic groups in the pre-Revolutionary era. A ledger covering a period that started in 1770 and has entries until 1795 lists the names of many prominent men in the area as guests along with their charges for liquor. It was on East Jersey Street, just across the way, that Governor Jonathan Belcher had his home, while Elias Boudinot IV, his father the silversmith, and other famous men of the day lived nearby. All of them are included in the ledger, which at last report was in the care of the Elizabeth Public Library.

When stagecoaches were in their heyday and the King's Highway (later St. George Avenue) was the most popular route to points west out of Elizabethtown, there was a tavern every few miles. To name them all would be a nearly impossible task. I will note only the most prominent.

Roselle

I remember to this day the old Wheat Sheaf Inn that stood for generations at the northwest corner of the highway and

Chestnut Street, leading north into what is present Roselle. My grandfather lived in that town from 1907 until his death in 1929, and many times I was in the family car when my father made the round trip to pay him a visit.

In those days a great part of St. George Avenue, and also Chestnut Street, ran through open country between towns. Now the countryside has been developed and the entire section is built up. The old tavern was torn down in the 1940s, after nearly two centuries of activity, to make way for a housing development. The Wheat Sheaf Inn was a stop for coaches to pick up passengers, but it always had to depend on carriage and wagon trade from neighboring Linden and other small villages, as well as on the local gentry.

Rahway

The Merchants and Drovers Tavern, still standing on St. George Avenue on the outskirts of Rahway at the intersection of the road leading to Westfield, was the first stop for stagecoaches bound for Philadelphia after leaving Elizabethtown in the morning. When John Mercereau's "Flying Machine" made its twice-weekly trip from Paulus Hook to Philadelphia over what was then called The King's Highway, this was the initial halt to change horses and pick up passengers.

Owned by descendants of John Anderson, who kept the tavern from the time of its building in the 1750s through 1775, the ancient wooden structure was renovated in the 1940s by F. C. Squire, great grandson of the original proprietor, and a member of an old family living along the avenue. It ceased to be a hostelry when the stage lines fell on evil days, and ceased even to have a license to serve liquor. Mr. Squire, the first not directly descended from the Andersons to own the premises, donated its free use to the Rahway Council of Girl Scouts.

Within recent months there has been a movement afoot to purchase the property by public subscription to save the structure from demolition in favor of a housing development. Anderson may have been the builder and first tavern operator, but otherwise little is known of its early history. It is known that the property came into possession of the Craig family through the marriage of Dr. David Stewart Craig to Phoebe, daughter of John Anderson. She died in 1883 at the age of ninety-three. The inn had been operated for well over a century by that time. After standing idle for years, it was acquired by Mr. Squire, who has since died without issue.

Mr. Squire, when I talked with him in the early 1940s, recalled a second building on the site. It was an exact duplicate of the present structure, he said, even to the kitchen extension and shed that stood beside it. There was a covered passageway between, he recalled.

My third grade teacher at old Scotch Plains grammar school was Miss Harriet Squire, a sister of Mr. Squire. That was more than sixty years ago. She had a remarkably keen memory and often told me stories of the tavern and St. George Avenue as they had been in her childhood. She once told me that prior to and during the Civil War, the inn was frequently filled with guests.

Miss Squire was a student of history generally, and of anything to do with St. George Avenue in particular. She noted that it was first called The King's Highway and was the only thoroughfare in Jersey connecting the Dutch on Manhattan Island with settlements on the Delaware River. It ran from Elizabethtown Point to the ford of the Raritan River at Inian's Ferry (New Brunswick), and on to the Delaware above Trenton. Early in the eighteenth century it was broadened and linked with the road running from the ferry at Amboy to Elizabethtown and Newark via Broad Street.

In King George's time on the throne of England, the road was extended across the meadows to Paulus Hook. At that time it was given the name of The King's Highway. Locally known as "the road to Bridgetown" (Rahway), it was used by Washington from New Brunswick to Elizabethtown on his way from Mount Vernon, Virginia, to New York to take the oath of office as the young republic's first president.

Miss Squire recalled witnessing many stirring scenes along St. George Avenue. She saw the entourage of President Benjamin Harrison in 1889 when he retraced the route taken by Washington in observance of the first centennial since that epic event.

Years later, when I had long been a member of the Sons of the American Revolution, I first learned that the journey of President Harrison in 1889 had led indirectly to the founding of the SAR. It seems that many Jersey residents belonged to the Sons of the Revolution and had long objected vociferously to the arduous trip to New York City to attend meetings.

The then Governor Green of New Jersey, who was a native of Elizabeth with a home right on St. George Avenue, was one of the rebellious members. He proposed that the group from *this* side of the Hudson River meet President Harrison along the avenue and stop at his home for luncheon. Everything went according to plan, and after a delightful repast all those present proceeded to Elizabethtown Point, where a six-oar flatboat was awaiting them, just as in Washington's time.

As the boat drew near the foot of Wall Street, the Jersey contingent of SAR members on board waved hands in greeting to the others assembled on the wharf. Next, the Jersey members held a meeting in Newark and decided to form a separate organization along more liberal lines. Thus began the Sons of the American Revolution, and Elizabeth, in deference to Governor Green, gained the distinction of having Elizabethtown Chapter Number One in the entire country, a distinction that it retains to this day.

New Brunswick

In New Brunswick, at Albany and Water Streets, there stood until 1970 the 200-year-old historic structure known for generations as the Indian Queen Tavern. A hospitable stop for travelers along the King's Highway, it played host to Washington, Adams, Franklin, and other famous men when the Republic was young.

Known in later years as the Colonial American Hotel, its location a step away from the Raritan River ferry crossing made it a natural point for weary travelers and farmers for miles around to stop for refreshment. Used as an inn and tavern bar almost continuously until a few years ago, it was finally abandoned for lack of business. Finally, it came within the path of development and was demolished to make room for an interchange designed to take traffic from Albany Street across the Raritan on Route 18, as the throughway has been renamed.

Who first operated the Indian Queen and the names of its later proprietors have been lost over the years. The most novel feature of construction was a spiral staircase rising from the first to the third floor, with thirty steps to the top. It was joined entirely by mortises and dowels.

Perth Amboy

In Perth Amboy the Long Ferry Tavern was just a step away from where the road originally crossed the Raritan River. The left portion of the structure was built in 1684 and the building was enlarged in the 1750s. During the Revolution it was a favorite resort for both townsmen and travelers.

Now left behind as the shore traffic speeds overhead on modern highways, it is sadly neglected. A movement has started locally to save the building before it is demolished.

There was a time when farmers around Middlesex County used the Long Ferry Tavern as a headquarters on the way to market. They parked their carts and wagons there and went on to New Brunswick, Elizabethtown, and Newark with their produce to sell. Boats were not large enough in those days to ferry horses and loaded wagons across. On the return trip the farmers stopped at the tavern for refreshment and frequently put up for the night before proceeding homeward.

Princeton

Princeton was another stop for stage lines along the King's Highway. Known at first as Prince Town, it was already a considerable village for those days, when the College of New Jersey (Princeton University) was removed from Newark in 1757. In 1749, according to the diary of a Professor Kalm now in the Princeton University Library, "most of the houses are built of wood and are contiguous, so that there are gardens and pastures between them."

Retaining much of its old charm to this day and reminding me of restored Williamsburg, Virginia, more than any other place north of the Mason and Dixon Line, Princeton was in two counties until 1838, when the present Mercer County was created by act of the New Jersey Legislature. Prior to that time, Naussau Street, the main thoroughfare, was the dividing line between Middlesex County and Somerset County, set apart from Middlesex in 1688. Until the outbreak of the Revolution in 1775, Princeton was in East Jersey, but the imaginary line separating it from West Jersey was so close that the difference was never considered important. As a matter of fact, Princeton was a full day out of Philadelphia on the stage route to New York, and weary travelers saw no need for taking such matters into account when seeking shelter for the night, nor did local citizens, nor farmers from the surrounding countryside. During and after the Revolution, Princeton took on added importance. More of that will be said in a later chapter.

There were really three taverns, or inns, in the Princeton of colonial times. The first was known at the start, and for many years thereafter, as the Sign of the New Jersey College (now Nassau Inn). In September 1753, William Mountere, who removed to Trenton later the same year, advertised in Philadelphia newspapers "a house and parcel of land in Princetown, East Jersey, for sale." Also described as a new house "near where the college is to be built," it was already in use as a tavern. In 1748, according to the deed now on file in Somerset County, Mountere purchased a piece of land on the north side of present-day Nassau Street. Today it is known far and wide as Nassau Inn, in charming Palmer Square across the street from the Princeton University campus.

The will of Thomas Leonard, dated December 5, 1755, and on file in Somerset County, describes the property as "the house and lot in Princetown where Samuel Horner now lives." Horner is recorded as keeping a tavern in the house as late as 1766, for on August 21 of that year the sheriff of Somerset County offered for sale, "at the tavern formerly kept by one Samuel Horner," the estate of George Campbell, including the Hudibras, another Princeton tavern of the colonial era.

The will of Samuel Horner is dated 1766, the year that John Reynell announced in Philadelphia papers that "the noted tavern at Princetown, where Samuel Horner now lives," was for rent. Apparently the tavern was taken over, whether by purchase or rent is not recorded, by William Hicks, a native of England. At that time it was still known as the Sign of the New Jersey College. The diary of Elizabeth

Drinker, now filed with Princeton University library, records for September 11, 1765, that the lady, while on a stage trip from Philadelphia to New York, "had breakfast at Hick's place in Princetown," but the location is not indicated.

In 1767 Hicks announced: "Mr. Barnhill's Machine (coach) uses the Subscriber's house, and Gentlemen having Goods or small Parcels to send to, or in the neighborhood of, Princeton may depend upon the utmost Care in forwarding or delivering them by the earliest Conveyance agreeable to directions." This is the first record I have found where the present name of Princeton is used.

It is also recorded in the Philadelphia papers of the time that stage lines "making the trip to New York, via Trenton, Princeton, where horses are changed at the Sign of the College, and Palles Hook" required two days—three days in the winter. The fare was ten shillings and three pence for each mile.

The New Jersey Medical Society was organized at the tavern, and the Trustees of the College of New Jersey chose it as the place to hold the official Commencement dinners each year in June. The cost for food at such gatherings was four shillings per plate in 1769, 1771, and 1772 (1770 is missing for some unaccountable reason), according to a paper on "The History of Nassau Inn at Princeton," prepared in recent years by a Professor Collins and now on file in the library of Princeton University. The cost of wines and other drinks averaged six shillings per person for those years.

In 1774 Hicks for a time managed the King's Arms Tavern at Perth Amboy, and later he moved on to the Province Arms Tavern in New York. He served in the latter post apparently for several years until he was removed by the British when they occupied the city.

Richard Stockton, member of a prominent family in the town and a member of the bar, advertised in Philadelphia and

New York newspapers on January 26, 1774, that "THE NOTED TAVERN, at the Sign of the College at Princeton, now kept by William Hicks, is to be LETT, and entered upon the FIRST of APRIL next."

Until early in 1776, the tavern was maintained by a William Whitehead. In that year it was taken over by Jacob G. Bergen. Its activities during and after the Revolution will be discussed later.

The Sign of the Hudibras was already operating as a tavern on what is now Nassau Street, near College Lane, in 1761. Newspapers of the time advertised for return of "a horse taken out of the Barrack or yard of Mr. Yard, tavern-keeper at Prince-Town, West Jersey, at the sign of the Hudibras." It referred, of course, to Joseph Yard, who left the tavern in 1762 to keep a Princeton store.

The next tavern keeper at the Sign of the Hudibras was George Campbell, who offered the place for sale in 1765, with the following details noted in advertisements in Philadelphia and New York papers:

Thirteen Good Feather Beds, plentifully furnished with Sheets, Pillow Cases and other Bedclothes, 13 Bedsteads, 7 of them with Sacking Bottoms, several Suites of very good Curtains, Table Linen, Towels, etc. Desks, Chests of Drawers, Dining and dressing Tables and Stands, Looking Glasses, a Variety of Chairs, such as Windsor Chairs, etc., Clothes Presses, several large and good Cupboards, Pictures, large and small; China and Delft Bowls, Dishes and Plates, Cups and Saucers, Decanters and Wine Glasses, Casters and Waiters, etc.; Several large and small Kitchen Tables, Iron Pots of all sizes, a large Brass washing Kettle, a large and good Pie Pan, large and small Brass and Copper tea Kettles and Coffee Pots, Brass and Iron Candlesticks and Snuffers, Pewter Dishes and Plates, Kitchen and Chamber Andirons, shovels and Tongs, a good roasting turn Jack and several Spits; Iron dripping and frying Pans and broiling Irons, both large and small; a good Coffee Mill, Salt and Knife Boxes, several good English Trammels, a Crane, Brass and Iron Chaffing Dishes, a good baking Stone, Sauce Pans, Cullenders, Bleekies [?] and Milk Pans.

Also advertised at the same time, but separately, was:

"The noted and well accustomed Tavern at the Sign of the Hudibras, at Prince-Town for sale, new with 12 rooms and 2 good Kitchens, 1 with a loft overhead with 2 rooms."

Abner Phillips was the next innkeeper at the Sign of the Hudibras. He was soon succeeded by Jacob Hier (Hyer), who declared in newspapers in 1768 that "the Stage-Waggons from New York to Philadelphia and back put up at my House." In January 1773, the tavern was burned down as a result of error on the part of a careless servant and for a time Hier kept his tavern in "the large yellow house opposite the college near Somerset Road," according to a local newspaper account, now yellow with age, of the time.

Hier was back at the old stand in a rebuilt tavern by the following November. According to old accounts, it had accommodations for forty guests, and thirty horses could be cared for at a single time.

The third Princeton tavern dating from colonial times was the King's Arms, kept for a short time by Jacob Hier before he moved over to the Sign of the Hudibras. The only reference I have found is in the New York *Mercury* in 1763, a copy of which is on file in the New York Public Library. In it George Norris advertises for sale "a house and lot near the college and the Presbyterian Meeting House at Prince-Town formerly kept by Joseph Morrow."

Trenton

The first tavern in Trenton, on the banks of the Delaware, dates from sometime in 1712. On April 1 of that year, according to records in the Mahlon Stacy house on the site and now maintained by the state, he sold a plot of ground on present-day State Street to William Yard. Yard was innkeeper until death came on December 8, 1744. During those early years, Yard's Inn was noted as the social center for the region and numerous public bodies designated it as their meeting place.

My mother was born in Trenton in 1876, the year of the centennial celebration. Her grandfather was Alpheus Byram, who kept Byram's Drugstore on State Street for many years and was an early resident.

The next application for a license for a tavern in Trenton was not filed with the Hunterdon County court until May 2, 1774, according to the record. The applicant was Joseph Clunn, who stated that he has "taken the House and Tavern known by the sign of the Ship and Castle." It was located on the northerly side of Front Street between the present Warren and Broad streets, next door to the Yard Tavern. The Clunn application would suggest that the Ship and Castle was then in existence, but diligent research has failed to confirm the date it began business, previous proprietors or, in fact, whether it was the village's second tavern. At any rate, the records indicate that it was discontinued around 1776, in the early days of the Revolution.

At the time of the Revolution there were four taverns in Trenton, according to an order by the Continental Congress of payment for provisions to various groups of Continental soldiers either passing through or raised in the village. I have already mentioned the first two. The third was on Warren Street fronting East Hanover Street, and was kept by a Charity Britton in the 1760s. The Black Horse Tavern was started originally in 1754 as the Ligonier, when James Rutherford bought the house and lot at Broad and State Streets formerly owned by Thomas Cadwalader and rented it to his nephew, Robert Rutherford, for a public place. According to a deed filed with the Hunterdon County Court dated July 27, 1759, title went to the nephew, who changed the name to that of a cavalry troop in which he once served.

Under the original name of Ligonier, the tavern and contents were advertised for sale on November 24, 1764, but it was not sold until six months later, when the purchaser was Robert Lettis Hopper, according to the still-existing record. Despite his financial difficulties, Robert Rutherford continued as owner until 1771, when it was again sold by the sheriff to John Johnson of Perth Amboy. In 1768 Rutherford turned operation of the place over to Rensselaer Williams, who changed the name to the Royal Oak. He even had a signpost painted of the towering oak tree that tradition says stood in front of the house. In 1773 Williams moved to a tavern at the Trenton Ferry and took the sign with him. After a hiatus of several years, the tavern resumed and, at least until 1776, it was kept by Rachel Stille, sister of a Loyalist. During the Revolution it sheltered many prominent personages, who will be discussed further on, along with other Trenton taverns that flourished during and after the Revolutionary period.

I have been reminded by Colonel Cleon E. Hammond of Schooley's Mountain of an old pre-Revolutionary map in the Rutgers University Library at New Brunswick. It is of the Princeton-Trenton-Pennington area, and near the present Route 31 (north from Trenton) and Bull Run Road (the Ewing Township line) a building is indicated on the map as Field's Tavern. It is the only tavern indicated, and yet there is not a trace of the structure now, nor do residents of the section know anything about such a place.

Englishtown

It is very likely that there were taverns in colonial times at both Middletown and Shrewsbury. Both places were settled shortly after Elizabethtown on March 7, 1683. There is no trace of a tavern in either town and we have to go to English-

Village Inn at Englishtown in 1973, dated 1732. COURTESY RICHARD M. LEA.

town before finding the Village House, erected along the main street in 1732. The county was the scene of many skirmishes and fights during the Revolution, including the Battle of Monmouth.

A few miles away, on the outskirts of Spring Lake, there is the modernized and still enchanting Old Mill. Built in 1720, it was originally a mill and retains the water wheel and lovely old millpond. Long operated as a tavern and shelter for travelers, it now serves food and drinks to motorists.

The York Road was not open across all of New Jersey until 1764. The portion in Pennsylvania, from Well's Ferry (now New Hope) to Philadelphia had been cleared a half century earlier, but it was not until travel between New York and the last-named town became too heavy for other routes that the high road opened its entire length.

The Jersey portion of the York Road ran from Elizabethtown Point, where it connected with ferries for New York, to Coryll's Ferry (Lambertville) on the Delaware, opposite Well's Ferry. It passed through such old pre-Revolutionary places as West Fields (Westfield), Scotch Plains, Bound Brook, Raritan, Centreville, Three Bridges, Larisonville, and Mt. Airy before reaching the Delaware.

Scotch Plains

There is not a trace of old inns, taverns, or other public houses until we reach present-day Scotch Plains. There, at the busy corner of Park Avenue and Front Street, still stands the Old Stage House Inn, as it is known for miles around. The center section was built in 1737, according to a date on the great stone fireplace, and it has been operated continuously as a public house except for a few years when it was a private residence.

Nearly thirty years ago the Fanwood-Scotch Plains Chapter, D.A.R., erected a bronze plaque on the triangle facing the structure, attesting to the fact that it was a regular stopping place for stages of the Swift Sure Stagecoach Lines operating over the York Road between Elizabethtown Point and Philadelphia. I was present at the time as president of the New Jersey Society, S.A.R.

The date of 1737 for the Stage House Inn is accepted by the New Jersey Historical Society.[1] It was a decade later

1. Proceedings of the New Jersey Historical Society for 1924, p. 113.

before Scotch Plains was settled by a band of Scotsmen who landed at Perth Amboy and moved northward to "just west of the West Fields of Elizabethtown."

The village came to be and still is known as Scotch Plains. For many years it was only a settlement in Fanwood Township, but legal status was established in 1929, when the Legislature passed an act changing the name to Scotch Plains Township. A Baptist Church was started in 1747, the year of settlement. It is second in America only to the Baptist church at Piscataway, and is the mother church of the first Baptist congregation on Manhattan Island. An early member was James Manning, who later became the first president of Brown University.

There was not much need for an inn at the start. Proof is lacking that the Stage House Inn was built originally for such a purpose, but there is no doubt that it is an interesting landmark. It is undoubtedly one of the oldest structures in the area. There were, however, few travelers in those years and the roads were extremely poor.

An eighteenth-century barn from the southern part of the township and a collection of early craft shops have been added to the Inn in a courtyard arrangement by Charles Detweiler, an architect who is the present owner. More will be said later about the Stage House Inn and other Scotch Plains taverns.

Raritan

On the main street of Raritan stands the Cornell house. The original portion was built as a tavern by George Middagh in 1734, even ahead of the York Road. The countryside had been settled largely by Dutch of the second generation from Long Island and they made Middagh's Tavern a center of activity. So far as I know, the tavern was only a stop on the

Swift Sure Stage Line and never served as a point for changing horses or sheltering passengers. The Middagh Tavern was smack on the imaginary line between East and West Jersey. In colonial times it drew farmers and others from both sides of the line and was the place where numerous sales and public meetings were held.

Bound Brook

Bound Brook, also on the York Road, is the oldest settlement in Somerset County, the first house having been built in 1683 by a Thomas Codrington. There is no trace of it today, although the town has a number of old buildings.

Near the Middlebrook, the west boundary of the town, was the Fisher Tavern, said to be the first to be established. The first Masonic Lodge in Somerset county was organized there, and during the Revolution George Washington, according to his diary, attended its meetings. On the south face of nearby First Mountain, the Continental Army was at Camp Middlebrook the winter of 1778-79 and Washington, with his headquarters at Somerville, roamed over the surrounding area.

Somerville

Somerville's first public house is said to have been Tunison's Tavern. There is no trace of it today, but the site at Main and Grove Streets is occupied by the Somerset Hotel. The proprietor of Tunison's Tavern was not a modest soul, for he advertised in the New York and Philadelphia papers that "this is the only tavern between New York and the setting sun."

Centerville

The overnight stop for coaches on the Swift Sure Stage Line was at Centerville near Readington, which in colonial times was known as Readings'. The tavern at Centerville stood at the road intersection opposite the village store. It has burned, but most of the original barn is standing. The rough clapboard sides have been covered by shingles for added warmth. It is now used as a community center and is appropriately marked.

Readington

At Readington, or Readings', there was a brief stop at the local tavern for coaches of the Swift Sure Stage Line, true also of the tavern at Reaville, a few miles further on and a sharp left turn to the west.

Ringoes

Ringo, the last stop on the York Road before entering Pennsylvania across the Delaware, had its first tavern in 1738. It is said to have been erected by Theopolis Ketchum, who also was its first keeper.

The first proof of a tavern here is the application of Philip Ringo to the county judge of Hunterdon for a license, in May 1738, to sell "spiritous liquor." The local justices and the Board of Freeholders for Hunterdon met at the tavern regularly until 1758 and the Sons of Liberty, whose members came from the lower part of the county, met there on March 18, 1766, according to old Hunterdon historians. John

Ringo, a son, succeeded to the management in 1750, and continued until 1779, when he joined the Continental Army.

Lambertville

Lambertville, long known as Coryll's Ferry, had its first tavern sometime after 1732. It was built by Emanuel Coryll, who in that year acquired the patent from John Powell, who in turn had purchased it from John Coats, the original patentee, in 1726. The tavern site was just below the present Lambertville-New Hope bridge across the Delaware.

In 1758 the death of Coryll, who had operated a ferry for "three miles up the Delaware and three miles down" besides keeping the tavern, left it to his widow, who leased the tavern to a son-in-law by the name of Philip Atkinson. He kept it until 1764, the year the York Road got started. A seizure of the property by the sheriff of Hunterdon resulted in a quick succession of landlords. In 1766 Robert Grant was the keeper. He carried on until 1770, when the tavern was taken over by a Captain Donald, who also operated the ferry. He moved to Frenchtown in 1775.

Stockton

Howell's Ferry (Stockton) was north of the York Road, and the tavern was a lively place during colonial times. It is said to have been started by a John Reading, who gave the ferry its first name, but the initial proof shows that a Daniel Howell was there in 1735. Undoubtedly he also changed the ferry name.

Various members of the Howell family appear as keepers of the tavern until 1772. In that year it was taken over by a Joseph Robeson, who had kept the ferry and tavern at Solesbury, just across the Delaware in Pennsylvania. He changed the name to Robeson's Ferry and tavern, and he carried on into the Revolution.

Byram

At Lower Black Eddy (Byram) was the Warford Tavern, according to an undated license application on file in old Hunterdon records. The tavern must have been started in colonial times by Aaron Warford, who stated his wish to cater to the needs of travelers from across the Deleware and also to the needs of the workers at several nearby fisheries. It probably dates from about 1739, when the place was known as the Point Pleasant Ferry.

Frenchtown

At Alexandria (Frenchtown), also north of the York Road, the first tavern was kept by a Luther Calvin in 1759. The place was patented to Robert H. Morris on April 29, 1746, according to Hunterdon records. Daniel Prigmore applied for a license for another house in May 1761, "near the place Luther kept many years."

Next, a tavern license application was filed by Absolom Runyon for his house "formerly kept by Daniel Pridmoe." In 1766 there came an application from William Fleming. Then, in 1774, an application was made by Samuel Fleming, which brings us into the Revolutionary period.

The so-called Blaine Room at the Coach N' Paddock, a present-day popular eating place on the outskirts of Clinton, in Hunterdon County, dates from 1685. Originally intended as a wayside stop and shelter for travelers between New York and Easton and other places along the Delaware River, it has undergone numerous changes, additions, and owners over the years. From a tavern it has in turn been a private dwelling, an inn, and finally a favorite stop for motorists wishing to dine amid colonial charm. There is a magnificent panorama of open fields and hills; the Perryville Room, and five fireplaces in various other rooms are also well worth seeing.

Ryland Inn, on the outskirts of Whitehouse along the road to Clinton, Phillipsburg, and Easton on the Delaware, is an entrancing wayside stop set amid century-old beech trees. The taproom and dining facilities have the high ceiling and long windows reminiscent of the long-forgotten Victorian era of a century and more ago. The original part of the house dates from the late 1600s, when it was a stopping place on the way to or from New York and Philadelphia.

Mount Bethel

The King George Inn stands on the main street of Mount Bethel, just across from the ancient Baptist meeting house, as it has since 1685. The road leads off the Old York Road, and for years the inn catered to travelers on the way to or from New York and Philadelphia as well as to farmers for miles around. At one time it was a winter-night stop for haying parties out of Plainfield, Watchung, and other nearby towns. Always operated as a tavern and hotel, it retains much of the original atmosphere and now functions as an attractive dining place. It is filled with authentic furnishings and curios accumulated over the years.

Besides the original taproom, there are open fireplaces in many of the rooms throughout the three-story native field-stone and narrow-clapboard structure. Bedchambers on the upper floors have been turned into living quarters for the owners and employees. A two-story veranda across the entire front facing the street adds a note of antiquity.

The King George Inn at Mt. Bethel, dating from 1682. Now a restaurant. Photographed in 1973.

4

Colonial Taverns in South Jersey

The first tavern in Burlington City and probably in all of South Jersey was a log cabin operated by a Dutchman even before the English came in 1675. Peter Jegou was the proprietor of what came to be known as Jegou's Tavern. It began sometime late in 1668 after he had obtained from Philip Careret a grant to land then called Leasy Point, at the juncture of Assincunk Creek and the Delaware River. Terms of the grant (East Jersey Deeds) allowed Jegou "to build and Keep a House of Entertainment for ye accommodation of Travelors."

Burlington

Jegou was not the first settler at Burlington. On May 14, 1678, according to East Jersey Deeds,[1] a certificate was issued over the signature of Governor Carteret to Cornelius Joris, Jurien Marcellis, and Jan Claessen, "then living at Lay Sei Point, opposite Matimicum Island."

The Burlington County Court records are missing prior to 1681, although Burlington City dates from 1677 and there

---

1. Libr. 8, p. 74, files of the New Jersey Historical Society.

were settlers before that time. Salem County, although settled before 1675, is in a similar situation. All its records after 1681 are in Burlington City, where the court met and had jurisdiction over all of West Jersey.

Gloucester County, originally much larger than it is now, dates from 1686, when it was created by the general assembly for West Jersey meeting at Burlington in response to a petition from early settlers. Thereafter courts met at Axwamus (Gloucester City). Atlantic County was organized in 1837 from Gloucester territory. Cumberland County was organized in 1747 and before that time had been part of Salem County. Cape May County really dates from 1609, when it was discovered by Henry Hudson; it gets its name from Cornelius Mey, who explored the coast in 1621 while employed by the Dutch West India Company, and was first organized in 1692. The first county courts, abandoned prior to the Revolution, were held the following year at New England Town.

There are numerous references to taverns and other "houses of public entertainment" in the first court records I have found. Diligent research has failed to find court records earlier than those for Burlington from 1681 to 1709, and I am satisfied that they are not a part of any files in the entire state. The Upland court met at first at Chester, Delaware, and had jurisdiction over Burlington and Salem counties in West Jersey. Those records have now been published, but they add nothing to the picture.

The earliest available Burlington court records reveal that on August 8, 1682, it took cognizance of what for those times were considered high prices for cider and rum. On August 19, 1729, the court issued a list of items and prices to be charged. This was for the benefit of both innkeeper and customers, and it will be discussed more fully in a succeeding chapter.

A license was granted Richard Basnett in June 1683 to operate a house "to sell Victals, Ale, Beere and Spirituous Liquors" for a period of one year. His tavern was on the south side of Water Street (now Delaware) on land he bought from John Hollinshead of the tall-clockmaking family, who had been licensed for the same purpose in 1680, according to the court papers.

Official committee and town meetings were held at the Basnett Tavern, according to town records, and at the time Basnett was a member of the General Assembly for West Jersey. After his death the tavern was kept by his widow, Elizabeth.

In 1697 the town fathers, meeting at the Basnett Tavern, voted to record Elizabeth Basnett and three other persons as keepers of "victualling houses" in Burlington City, as follows:

> The Burgess of ye towne of Burlington exhibit to ye Court ye Recognizance of Elizabeth Basnett, Henry Rambo, Thomas Kendall and George Willis for ye Keeping of Victualling Houses.

The motion was approved by the court and ordered to be placed on file.

Sometime before 1721, Thomas Hunlock became proprietor of the Basnett Tavern and in that year, according to town records, he was granted a patent by Governor Burnet to keep a ferry on the Delaware from Burlington to New Bristol, for one mile in either direction. It obviously was not the first ferry, because the grant states that "it had not previously been well attended." Then, in 1725, Hunlock had become sufficiently well known in the area to be appointed high sheriff at Burlington City. That same year the tavern was offered for rent in Philadelphia papers as "a large brick house, now occupied by Colonel Thomas Hunlock, in Burlington." It was taken over on a three-year basis by William Bagley, whose will, written in 1727, describes him as "an innkeeper."

After Hunlock's duties as sheriff ended and the rental had expired, he again took over the tavern. In 1742 he advertised in Philadelphia papers of the loss of a "Small Ferryboat that has either been Stolen or Set Adrift in the River." It was described as fourteen feet long with a beam of five and one-half feet. In 1745, by which time the name had been changed to The Sign of the Angel, the vestry of St. Mary's Episcopal Church met at the tavern and closed title on behalf of the parsonage—the property at what are now Broad and Talbot Streets.

Hunlock died later in 1745 and his widow, Elizabeth, carried on until her death in 1748, when a son, Bowman Hunlock, took over. Other innkeepers mentioned in town and court records include Thomas Staples, Jr., Christian Finigan, and George Hulme.

The most famous of Burlington's colonial public houses was the Blue Anchor Tavern, originally erected in the 1740s by Richard Smith and still standing, although much altered, at Broad and High Streets. Known in later years as the City Hotel, Belden House, and finally the Metropolitan Inn, it won great renown during and after the Revolution, of which more will be said later.

Although Smith built the Blue Anchor Tavern, the first actual keeper was Thomas Shreve. His descendant, Donald Shreve, lived for years in Fanwood, then retired long ago to Pennsylvania. He told me on one occasion that his ancestor quit early to join the local militia, becoming a major in the Revolution.

Fretwell Wright advertised in 1751 that he was keeping the Blue Anchor Tavern and that a stagecoach "kept by Fretwell Wright at the Blue Anchor in Burlington and by John Predmore in Cranberry will go from Burlington to New York and return." The length of time required for the trip, hours of departure, and price were also stated.

John Shaw was proprietor in 1757 when the Burlington court, according to its records, adjourned to his house, but it is not stated from where it adjourned. He died in 1776 under strange circumstances, and was succeeded by Archibald Mc-Elroy, who lasted only a brief time. Under the tenancy of James Edsall, the Blue Anchor Tavern became headquarters for members of the New Jersey militia and entered the Revolutionary era.

Another colonial tavern was one kept by Henry Grubb in 1681, when he was first granted a license. It stood at Pearl Street and Delaware Avenue. According to the Burlington Township committee records:

> Burlington, the 19th of the 11th mo. 1704/5—At the Town Meeting held at the Town House and then adjourn to Henry Grubbs—.

In those days various town groups and the courts had a habit of meeting at or adjourning to public houses. It was so noted in the record.

The Stage Boat Tavern was another colonial public house in Burlington. It was first opened by Peter Baynton about 1743 on the river side of Delaware Avenue, near the Basnett Tavern. Soon it was kept by Patrick O'Hanlon, who was succeeded in 1750 by Jonathan Thomas, and soon it became the starting and stopping place for "stages bound for the Amboys."

Early in 1758 Thomas was succeeded by Joseph Hollingshead, another member of the tall-clockmaking family. Meetings of the General Assembly of West Jersey were held at the Hollinshead house in 1758-59, according to warrants drawn to his order for rent, heat, and food. These warrants are part of the General Assembly records.

The last colonial proprietor of the Stage Boat Tavern was Joseph Haight. He changed the name temporarily to the Sign of the General Wolfe, in honor of the man who commanded at Quebec. That was before 1770, when it reverted to the old name.

Still another Burlington public house of the colonial period was the tavern at High and Broad Streets, first a matter of history in 1732, when James Moon is recorded as licensee. Aaron Lovett and John Butcher, Jr., are listed as later license holders and during the period from 1785 to 1794, when Isreal Tonkins kept the place, it was known as the Washington House.

Crosswicks

The Crosswicks settlement is known to have had an inn as early as 1689, because in that year the court at Burlington revoked the license of John Bainbridge, according to its records, for selling rum to the Indians. At that time Crosswicks included a large territory and the precise location of the Bainbridge tavern is unknown.

The next mention of Crosswicks in the early record is a 1743 advertisement in a Philadelphia paper, when Joseph Borden offered a house and lot for sale. I do not know whether it was the same house that Bainbridge had operated earlier, but it is stated that "the House has been a Public House for many years past and is conveniently situated for that purpose, it being on the King's High Road." Apparently there was no sale, because a license was issued by the court at Burlington in May 1744 to Thomas Douglass, a son-in-law of Borden. He kept the tavern until his death in 1768 and then a son, Joseph, took over through the Revolution.

Bordentown

At Bordentown the earliest tavern of record was one kept by John Moor. As far back as 1703, he is recorded as keeping such a place in his house. On one occasion the town meeting of Chesterfield shows in its minutes the payment of 15.0.9 to him for board and care for an indigent resident. He died in 1735. The precise location of his tavern is unknown.

John Richards was licensed by the Burlington court in 1742 to keep a tavern at Bordentown. In 1744 the sheriff at Burlington reported to the court that the had seized a dwelling, outbuildings, and furnishings belonging to a "Joseph Richards and known as the Sign of the Punch Bowl, to a value unknown" in accordance with a writ issued by the court as result of a suit filed against Richards. Whether he was a father or brother of John, or whether it is merely an error in the first name (not unusual in those days) is unknown. At any rate, it is the sole mention of the Sign of the Punch Bowl Tavern that I have found, except for the fact that Abigail Hall, John Thorn, and Thomas Hay are listed as successive licensees until 1760, when it ceased operating.

Brown's Tavern is definitely known to have been located at the intersection of Main and Crosswicks Streets in 1725, and it was kept at that time by a Dr. Joseph Brown, a son-in-law of Joseph Borden, after whom Bordentown got its name.

In his autobiography Benjamin Franklin tells of spending the night at "an inn, within eight or ten miles of Burlington, kept by one Dr. Brown" whom he accused of vilifying the Bible in doggerel verse.

Franklin, on his way by boat from Boston to New York, thence overland to the Amboys and so to Brown's Tavern, proceeded the next morning to Burlington, where he tarried long enought to aid as a printer before going on to his final destination in Philadelphia, according to the account in his autobiography. More of that later.

The names of various innkeepers and licensees of Brown's Tavern appear in the court record, from John Clayton in 1730 until George Applegate during and after the Revolution.

Mount Holly

Mount Holly, one of Burlington County's first settlements, dating from 1681, had a tavern as early as 1737, according to old records. It stood on the north side of Mill Street, near the intersection with Buttonwood Street. The first proprietor and also owner of the property was John Odgen, a member of the old Elizabethtown family of that name. He was succeeded by a Thomas Atkinson, who is recorded also as a major owner of the gristmill that was directly across the street. He was succeeded in 1754 by George Windsor, according to records of the county court at Burlington. Following his death in 1758, all trace of the house is lost, although local tradition has it that his widow carried on for a time.

Mount Holly's most famous tavern is still standing on Mill Street near the intersection with Pine Street, although it is much changed over the years. Started in late 1754 by Thomas Atkinson, who left the nearby establishment, it was called the Three Tun Tavern. Atkinson continued until 1757, when he was succeeded by Zachariah Rossell until 1765. In that year, according to court records of licenses granted, he went to the Cross Keys Inn at Burlington, and Daniel Jones, who had been at that place, went to the Three Tun Tavern.

The unusual name of the tavern has never been explained. In 1759 advertisements in Philadelphia and New York papers of the time (the first paper in New Jersey began twenty years later) announced a stage line formed to travel the Monmouth Road between Philadelphia and New York by way of Moorestown, Mount Holly, and Middletown.

Other colonial taverns in Mount Holly, the license records of the court sitting at Burlington show, were the house of John Burr, Jr., first licensed in 1749; the Black Horse Tavern; started by John Adams in 1746; and the Cross Keys Tavern, kept by Thomas Clark, who died in 1731.

Columbus

The first regularly licensed tavern at Black Horse (Columbus) was operated by Thomas Kerlin from 1745 until 1748, after which there is no record. Richard Cox, who opened the Black Horse Tavern, was granted a license in 1761. After three years at a place called Mansfield in the Columbus area on the road from Burlington to Wrightstown, he announced removal to Trenton.

While on the subject of Mansfield, I shall refer to the Crooked Billet Tavern in Mansfield Township, along the road from Burlington to Bordentown. The first license was issued to Isaac Gibbs in 1746. He was followed by a son until 1758, when John Horner took over. He was succeeded in 1761 by John Butler, Sr., who is recorded as "lately of Nottingham Township." He and a son remained until 1770, when Solomon Rockhill took over and remained during the Revolution.

The Rising Sun Tavern, on the road running through Mansfield Square on the way to Georgetown, was kept as early as 1761 by Thomas Atkinson. Joseph Archer took over in 1772 for the Revolutionary War period until 1780. He was indicted in 1774, according to Burlington court records, for allowing gambling on the premises, but his license was renewed each year.

Tuckerton

The first tavern keeper at Tuckerton, which since 1891 has been in Ocean County, was Joseph Gaunt, who was licensed in July 1769. He was followed in 1774 by Reuben Tucker as keeper of the tavern on Main Street near Wood Street.

Tuckerton Township, whose boundaries were defined by the court at Burlington at the May 1741 term, is very often confused with Little Egg Harbor. Actually it is on Tuckerton Creek, which leads into Little Egg Harbor Inlet and so to the Atlantic Ocean.

Another colonial tavern in Tuckerton was opened by Caleb Evans, also in 1769, in a frame building that stood a few doors north of the present Carlton Hotel. The Carlton Hotel was formerly known as the Union Hotel and was not established until about 1819, judging from the first license application.

Arneytown

The only other colonial tavern in what was once the vast region of Burlington County was the house at Arneytown located on the Province Line Road, now the boundary between Burlington and Monmouth counties. At one time on the boundary between East and West Jersey, it is one of the oldest now standing; when I last saw it in 1970, it was sadly in need of repair. Only a few dilapidated buildings and a scant dozen residents are all that is left of a once-thriving village of several hundred souls.

Once known as the Lawrie House, the tavern was built in 1731 by William Lawrie, a pioneer in the area, although the first license application of record was not filed until 1762. According to local tradition, the keeper at that time was a Richard Potts, son-in-law of Joseph Arney, after whom the village was named. Records in the New Jersey State Library at Trenton tell a different story. They indicate that a Richard Platt was landlord in 1762, and he is listed as a son-in-law of William Lawrie. Later on, a man named Willis is listed as owner.

On a rafter may be seen the following inscription:

March 12, 1765. Mary Forsythe, James doth love.

Because of the tavern's unique location on the mythical line between East and West Jersey, it was used many times by the sheriffs of Burlington and Monmouth counties as a place to hold sales of land and other chattels. It was the gathering place for citizens from the surrounding country in the latter part of the eighteenth century, and the first stop for stage coaches en route from the Delaware across the state.

It is recorded that John Darby was local postmaster in 1827. He served until the post office closed for good on February 9, 1871.

As it now stands, the ancient tavern is two-and-one-half stories high, with a one-story extension. Its exterior walls are clapboard over a stone foundation. The roof has pitch and tin over wooden shingles. The interior walls are of paneling part way to the ceiling, with plaster above.

Two white columns frame the front entrance door, which is protected by a large peaked roof. A Dutch-type door at the right of the inside hallway leads to the kitchen and has the old latch and strap hinges. There is a walk-in fireplace in the kitchen and a narrow brick hearth. The crane and hinge hanging in the fireplace are said to be the originals.

The public room, where the sheriff and other sales are said to have been held, has dark wood paneling from the floor halfway to the ceiling. Above that there is plaster. There are also a storage and dining room on the first floor, plus a large parlor, all across a central hall from the taproom and kitchen. On the second floor there are six bedrooms. In a corner of the dining room is a cupboard with double solid doors at the top and doors with rectangular panes at the bottom. It is the special pride of William H. Grover, the present owner.

There was a tavern at Bridgeboro, near the Rancocas Creek, in 1755. The proprietor was William Allen, according to the license application, and he continued until 1769, after which Samuel Laconey appears as the licensee. A second tavern at Bridgeboro was opened by Thomas Gill in 1763.

John Wilkinson was keeping the Cooperstown Tavern on the Burlington Pike, on the way to Beverly, as early as 1772. He was succeeded in 1774 by Peter Wilkinson, who is shown on the license application as "a friend."

In a place once called Slabtown and later Jacksonville, a house located on the road from Mount Holly to Shreveville (now Smithville) was kept in 1750 by Joseph Richards, whose various applications are dated in 1750, 1751, and 1752, and again in 1768-69.

Wrightstown

Job Lippencott, Jr., was licensed in 1747 to keep a public house at Jobstown, on the road from Monmouth to Wrightstown and New Egypt. He filed applications each year thereafter until 1759, when he died and a son took over until 1766. Then John Hutchins followed.

The Juliustown pioneer tavern keeper was Reuben Eldridge. That was in 1761 and not another license application was filed until after the Revolution.

The Wrightstown Tavern was kept from 1753 to 1762 by John Wright. He was succeeded by Joel Ware.

It has been stated previously that all records of Burlington County, which included Salem County until 1706, were lost prior to 1681. Before that time the court met at Upland (New Castle, Del.), and for that reason some of the earliest land grants and deeds are on file there. Thus all petitions and license applications from 1681 to 1706 are to be found as part of the Burlington court record, even though many of them pertain to what is now Salem County.

After September 1706, the Salem County court met at Salem Town. It handled all license requests within its boundaries, extending along the Delaware River from Swedesboro southward to a point near Salem Creek.

Salem Town

Probably the first tavern keeper within the present Salem County was a Dutchman by the name of Fopp Jansen Outhout. He was licensed by Governor Carteret on March 25, 1669, to maintain a tavern at an unnamed place. He was granted a patent by the governor on May 3, 1669, to a piece of land on the Jersey side of the Delaware that he had purchased previously from the Indians. According to Christopher Ward, author of *The Dutch & Swedes on the Delaware, 1609-1664,* Outhout was still keeping the tavern in 1679.

Charles S. Boyer, a student of South Jersey who died in 1936, puts the Outhout tavern at Bouttown, now Carney's Point, and said that in 1676 Outhout was one of the signers of the Concessions and Agreements of the West Jersey Proprietors. Also, according to Boyer, the court at Salem issued regulations to control inns and taverns in 1709, 1718, and again in 1729. They not only regulated the credit amounts to be allowed customers, but, Boyer says, fixed the prices of liquor and victuals.

The Salem County Historical Society is responsible for much of the information concerning the county's early public houses. A pamphlet in its keeping published several years ago says that the first tavern keeper in Salem Town was William Hall, according to a deed dated August 17, 1692. The pamphlet places the Hall tavern at the foot of Broadway and says it is known now as Broadway House.

The second tavern in Salem Town was kept by James Ridley, according to the society. It is known now as the Mecum Building at Broadway and Walnut Street. Ridley died in late 1705, according to a will on file in Burlington City, although in 1703 the tavern was sold to a William Griffen. Griffen is noted as an innkeeper in 1722, in papers on file with the Salem County court, when he was allowed twenty shillings for use of his house by the court when it was in session.

The next tavern keeper named by the society was Benjamin Haynes, who was granted a license by the court meeting in Salem Town in 1727. It was renewed annually until his death in 1733, when his widow, Anne Haynes, took over. The last license of record was granted to her in 1744.

James Wiggins, whose property adjoined that of Haynes and is mentioned in the latter's will on file in Salem County, had a license each year from 1757 until 1761, when he, too, died. Other licenses granted by the Salem court without identifying the locations, were to William Crabb in 1741, Abner Penton in 1746, Richard Craven in 1741, William Murdock in 1742, Daniel Smith in 1744, Elizabeth Smith (perhaps his widow) in 1751, and Daniel Mestayer in 1734 and again in 1735.

John Jones conducted a tavern in Salem Town for years, starting in 1739, according to license applications on file with the Salem County court. He had been clerk to the county's Board of Freeholders prior to and subsequent to that time. Notations appear on the board records of his reimbursement for meetings held at his house. His death in 1740 resulted in his widow, Elizabeth Jones, taking over until 1747, and board records indicate that meetings continued at the tavern.

Thomas Rice applied for a license to keep an "Antient House" in 1747. In the absence of a named location, I conjecture that it was the same place formerly kept by the Widow Jones. At any rate, Rice appears to have continued until 1755, when others succeeded, until finally John Dickinson took over in 1761 and continued until his death in 1777. Over the years the place came to be known as Dickinson's Tavern and was a prominent coach stop.

Other early applications for public houses in Salem Town included one in 1739 for Sherron's Tavern at the head of

Market Street, and another in November 1758 for the Joseph Burrough's Tavern at Market Street and Broadway.

Other Salem County public houses of the colonial era included the Alloway Tavern kept by Joseph Thompson in 1753, according to his license application in that year. A brother of the Benjamin Thompson who managed the nearby Casper Wistar glass works over the same period, he continued annual renewal requests until his death on October 20, 1776, according to a copy of his will filed with the Salem County Court seeking a probate. Biddle's Tavern on Salem Creek was kept by William Biddle in 1761, application records indicate, and he continued until his death in 1771. A son kept the tavern through the Revolution. Charles Dayton sought and was granted a license in 1763 to keep the Centerton Tavern in the Piles Grove Township "on the road from Cumberland County to Grate Eggharbor."

Daretown

A tavern at present-day Daretown in Salem County was kept by Mounce Keen, whose license application, dated 1749, states that the house where he then lived had been a tavern "for many Years past." After 1760 he was followed from 1761 to 1770 by Richard Sparks. In the latter year the keeper is shown as Jacob Elwell. Thomas Sparks is listed as keeper of a Daretown tavern in 1756, continuing until 1763, when a son, Robert, took over until midway in the Revolution.

Peter Duffill filed an application in August 1747 to be licensed for a tavern "on the road from Burlington to Cohansey & from Cohansey to Salem." He was succeeded in 1757 by Jacob Freas, who had many endorsers and continued each year until 1784.

Hancock's Bridge

The earliest application for a tavern at Hancock's Bridge, also in Salem County, was filed by Samuel Baker in 1761. A tavern at Penn's Neck was established late in 1733 by Peter Insloe, according to a license application dated August 3 of that year. In 1743 he was succeeded by Allen Congleton.

The first record of a tavern at Pennsville is a license application dated June 1746, filed by Archibald Crawford. Following his death in 1748, his widow, Catherine, took over and in 1754 August Miller became proprietor. In 1758 Philip Alexander filed for a license and was followed by Edmond Doughtery in 1762, by the latter's widow until 1770, and then by Robert Kitts.

The Pole Tavern, which was also known as Champney's, on the road to Daretown, was first licensed in 1770 by Joseph Champney, who was granted a license in that year. He died in 1773, the records show, and his widow took over until 1778.

The Pumpkin Tavern, on the road from Harmersville, was first licensed in 1750 by James Stretch, although it is said to have been built as early as 1730. The first tavern at Remsterville was probably started before 1761, when William Craig filed his initial request for a license. A short mile out of Alloway and also on the road to Freasburg, it was near the Casper Wistar glass house established in 1739 and was kept by Craig, who is said to have purchased an adjoining gristmill from Wistar, until 1773, when the last renewal was granted.

Swedesboro

The Sculltown Tavern on the road from Swedesboro to Pennsville was opened in 1759, and the next year the proprietor's widow applied for a renewal before selling the place to

Abel Harris in 1762. License applications were filed by other proprietors before the Revolution and the village is now called Auburn.

In February 1750 Abraham Nelson applied for a license to keep the Seven Star Tavern "on the King's Highway" between Swedesboro and Sharptown. The accompanying petition stated that the signers saw "a Great Necessity for a Publick House in the Neighborhood by Reason of Travellers Suffering and also Impose on Private Houses or Suffer greatly." His son, Joseph, became keeper until 1756, when he was succeeded until 1762 by John Sparks "late of Gloucester County." The original tavern stood on land sold to Peter Louderbach in 1762, on which he later built a brick house (still standing), applying for his first license in 1770. He kept the place until death came in 1780.

The old Lambson House at Stone Island, on the Salem River in Lower Penn's Neck Township, is still standing. It was built, according to local tradition, in 1741, but the first license record for Mathias Lambson is dated in February 1753. After three years he leased to a man named Solomon Lloyd, and in another three years, when the lease expired, Hance Lambson filed for a license. The relationship of Hance to Mathias is not explained.

The Wistarburg Tavern, on the road to Pilesgrove from Alloway, adjoined the Wistar glass house and was a natural for the workmen who labored at the glass house and lived close by. The first tavern keeper was Lodowick Hall, and his initial license was granted in 1741, two years after the glass house started operations. A license "to operate a tavern at Pilegrove" was granted in 1771 to Jacob Paullin, although whether it was for the same house is not known.

Woodstown

The first tavern in Woodstown was kept by Obadiah

Lloyd, whose license request was approved in 1721. Applications were filed each year up to 1750. John Lloyd, probably a son or perhaps a nephew, filed in 1762 and in 1768 his son apparently took over. In 1740 Samuel Graves sought a license to keep a tavern in his house on the Salem road out of Woodstown. In 1769 John Brierley was granted a license for a house in Woodstown known later as Barber's Tavern, after Samuel Barber, who took over after a few years and remained through the Revolution.

The first tavern in Gloucester County was opened in December 1693, which was seven years after the county was formed in 1686, according to a resolution adopted by the General Assembly meeting at Burlington. It was probably located on the site of present-day Haddonfield, and the applicant was Henry Treadway. His application requested a continuance of license, thus indicating previous operation. At the same term of court, Isaac Hollingham and Edward Burrough applied for permission "to keep ordinaries" in the village.

In 1837, as before stated, Atlantic County was carved out of Gloucester County, followed by Camden County in 1845. The colonial taverns hereafter mentioned were in these two counties.

Gloucester Town

In December 1692 the first license request was filed with the court by Matthew Medcalfe, an early settler of Gloucester Town. George Webb, the court minutes show, was at the same time granted permission to keep a tavern in the village. Renewals were sought each year by Medcalfe until 1701, except for the period when he was high sheriff of Gloucester County, and that is covered by the license application of Thomas Norrice dated July 13, 1698.

Other early taverns in Gloucester Town were kept by persons who later moved to various parts of the country, records indicate.

Camden

Hugg's Tavern—standing until 1927, when it was torn down by the park commission of Camden County—is said to have been built in 1720 by Joseph Hugg. He was granted a license on November 26, 1722, to operate a ferry to Philadelphia and, at the same time, to keep the tavern. Hugg died in 1731 and his son, William, then only fourteen years of age, could not take over until 1741. In the meanwhile his mother became the administrator and carried on herself at first, then with a succession of innkeepers.

William Hugg died in 1775 and his son became tavern keeper. The father had achieved prominence in county affairs and his establishment is mentioned often in early records of the Board of Freeholders. The Gloucester Fox Hunting Club, one of the first in the entire country, was organized there in 1766.

Tel-News, a publication of the New Jersey Bell Telephone Company, is authority for the statement that John Ross, over two hundred years ago, on November 4, 1773, married his sweetheart, Betsey Griscom of Philadelphia, at Hugg's Tavern. He was a local upholsterer. She gained fame, as a widow, when General George Washington commissioned her to make the first all-American flag. It was flown for the first time over American troops at Camp Middlebrook, in back of Bound Brook, in the Watchung Mountains, when Washington's troops were in winter quarters there and he was at nearby Somerville, with headquarters in the Wallace house.

Woodbury

The court records for September 1700 show that Stephen Jones was granted a license to keep a tavern at Woodbury and in 1710 John Tatem was licensed to operate a ferry and keep a tavern on one side of the crossing at Woodbury Creek. William Tatem, probably a son, was licensed later, and about 1741 Henry Sparks, "late of Gloucester Township," took over.

John Tatem was licensed for 1747 and 1748 to keep the Upper Tavern across from the Quaker meetinghouse in Woodbury. A son, Joseph, kept the tavern from 1751 until 1774, when his son came in during the Revolution.

The so-called Middle Tavern in Woodbury, known after the Revolution as the Washington House, was licensed first in 1748, with Abraham Chattin as innkeeper, according to his application filed with the Gloucester County court. He had kept at least one tavern previously in Woodbury, because early records of the Board of Freeholders show that on August 28, 1738, he submitted a bill for food and drink. James Wood was the proprietor, and in 1759 John Hillman was licensed. In 1772 he was followed by Jehu Wood.

Benjamin Cooper was granted a license in 1727 to keep a tavern at the Jersey side of a ferry to Philadelphia operated by his father from Cooper's Point (Camden). Renewals were each year until 1761, when Bradford Roberts applied for a license. He kept on until 1763, and the next year the place appears to have been taken over by Samuel Cooper. After renewals each year for five years, he next appllied for a license to run a new tavern and also a ferry he had constructed a hundred yards below the old site.

William Royden gained a license in 1693 to operate a tavern in his house, which stood on Cooper Street between the present Point Street and Delaware Avenue. It was taken over in 1741 by Daniel Cooper and came to be known for years thereafter as Cooper's Tavern.

Another Cooper tavern was at the foot of Federal Street. The first license issued by the court, then meeting at

Axwamus (Gloucester City), was to Joshua Cooper, although the house in which it operated had been built by Daniel Cooper. It was finally demolished near the end of the last century, but over the years and under nearly a score of land-lords, according to the court records, it was headquarters for numerous politicians, lawyers, and others who picked local officials, governors, and even members of Congress.

Arthur Donaldson was issued a license in 1765 to keep a tavern at Kaighn's Point, now at Kaighn Avenue and Front Street, in present-day Camden. It was in a house previously erected by Joseph Kaighn, who occupied it during the Revolution as a private dwelling, it is reported.

Haddonfield

Haddonfield had its earliest tavern in 1733, although the town dates from 1683. Thomas Perry Webb was issued a license for it each year until 1741, when his widow applied each year until her death in 1750. Robert Price then became landlord until 1758. He was succeeded by no less than five applicants for licenses before the Revolution.

Haddonfield's second colonial tavern was kept by a woman, Sarah Norris, who was licensed in 1741. The tavern stood on present-day Main Street, near Potter Street. She continued each year until June 1746, when John Jones was licensed to "keep the house wherein Sarah Norris late kept." Sarah Norris again took over for a time in 1750. There are three other names shown on applications before the Revolution, during which period the innkeepers apparently included Hugh Creighton, who took over in 1759. In the *Pennsylvania Gazette* for September 22, 1768, I have found an advertisement for a "fuller or sheerman," instructing applicants to apply at "the field," a name adopted by Creighton. Later, he appears to have taken over a building now standing as part of

Indian King Tavern at Haddonfield, dating about 1750. This was the meeting-place of the State Legislature in 1777, and where the State Seal was adopted. Photographed in 1972. COURTESY NEW JERSEY DEPARTMENT OF ENVIRONMENTAL PROTECTION.

a larger structure. Built in 1750 by Mathias Aspden, a wealthy Philadelphia merchant, it is where the great seal of New Jersey was first received and adopted by the state's assembly. Now owned by the state and open by appointment, the old tavern is marked by a plaque donated by the D.A.R.

On the outskirts of Clarksboro, on the road from Woodbury, a tavern was kept by Christopher Taylor in 1727. Along the famed King's Highway and later known as Death of the Fox Tavern, it was offered for sale in the *Pennsylvania*

Gazette in 1731 apparently without success, because Taylor joined with other tavern keepers in 1733 to protest the imposing by the assembly to Gloucester Town of a tax on all "the keepers of Public Houses" to support the government. Benjamin Peters applied for a license to keep the place in 1734. At least a dozen other innkeepers applied for licenses to keep the place before the Revolution.

Bridgeport

Bridgeport, on Lower Raccoon Creek, had its first tavern in 1740, according to an application for a license filed in March of that year by James Boucher. Timothy Rain applied in 1751. In 1764 Benjamin Howell applied for a license to conduct a tavern and ferry at a point "on the Delaware opposite Marcus' Hook." He died in 1766 and his widow carried on into the Revolution.

Numerous other applications for licenses to operate taverns during the colonial era in what was then Gloucester County are matters of court record. They include that of Robert Gerrard for the Blue Bell Tavern in 1724, another by William Lindsey in 1752 for the famed Pine Tavern "on the Cohawking Road outside Pineville," and one by Thomas Wilkins, in 1736, to keep the Upper Tavern outside Swedesboro.

As early as 1751, travel from Philadelphia via the three ferries at Cooper's Ferry (Camden) and thence along the White Horse Pike had become so great that the White Horse Tavern was licensed at a special town meeting in Gloucester. It is still standing after surviving many changes in tavern keepers and now caters to motor traffic along the old pike.

Bridgeton

Bridgeton, originally known as Bridgetown, had several

early taverns. The first was licensed by Silas Parvin in 1737. It stood a bit south of the present Commerce street and was kept by him until 1764, when tradition has it that he quit to devote full attention to the general store he had operated since 1731. Captain Elias Cotting kept a tavern near Broad Street from 1741 to 1743 and John Hall was licensed from 1756 until 1767 to keep "Hall's Tavern near the Courthouse." Hall's tavern was destroyed by a fire in 1758, which also burned the courthouse, and while both were rebuilding, meetings of the Board of Freeholders, according to old records, were held at Keen's Tavern, which had been licensed in 1754.

Cape May County, discovered by Henry Hudson on August 28, 1609, and again in 1621, when Cornelius Mey explored the coast, undoubtedly had colonial taverns, but, alas, we have only the very old court records to go by and they do not give locations of such public houses.

Taken from Salem County on November 12, 1692, Cape May County extended from the upper reaches of the Maurice River to the shores of Little Egg Harbor. The first grand jury of the court, meeting at Town Bank on the Delaware, was to regulate the sale of liquors, which is another indication that taverns existed. Town Bank, also known in early times as New England Town and Cape May Town, had been settled in 1685 by whalers from Cape Cod and Long Island.

Cape May City

Town Bank was abandoned before the Revolution when whaling ceased to be profitable, and Cape May City, dating from 1690, became the leading settlement. Records start with "a town meeting held May 10, 1692, at the house of Benjamin Godfrey," and it is likely that he was, or became, the county's first tavern keeper.

The first license granted by the court for Cape May

County was on the application of Jacob Ludlum, Jr., dated in 1740. According to Salter's *A History of Monmouth and Ocean Counties*, it is the first license to operate a tavern on record in the county.

According to accounts in the Philadelphia and Trenton papers of the time, the Jacob Gibbs Inn, which stood for many years in the early eighteenth century at Fort Billingsby, a few miles down the Delaware from Fort Mercer, was long a popular stopping place "for coaches enroute from Trenton and points north to Philadelphia and places in southern New Jersey."

Nesco

The Sailor Boy Hotel at present-day Nesco, in Burlington County, was established earlier than 1781, when it is first mentioned as the place where Joseph Mulliner, a notorious robber of the time, was captured. Retaining much of its colonial charm, it is now used as a private residence. In his book on old taverns in South Jersey, Boyer places it on the stage road between the Delaware River and the Atlantic Ocean, about 25 miles from Atlantic City. He says the first owner was William Coffin, and in 1805 it was purchased by Isaac Bolton. He also says that the tavern signboard depicted a sailor, painted in blue, with white cap.

A *New Jersey Gazette* of 1781 on file with the New Jersey Historical Society in Newark, says:

> At a special Court lately held in Burlington, a certain Joseph Mulliner of Egg-Harbour was convicted of high treason and is sentenced to be hanged this day. This fellow had become the terror of that part of the country. He had made a practise of burning houses, robbing and plundering all who fell in his way, so that when he came to trial it appeared that the whole country, both Whigs and Tories, were his enemies.

5

Inns and Houses
during the Revolution and After

During the Revolution, from 1775 until 1783, most of the colonial taverns and numerous public houses set up in New Jersey in those stirring days did a thriving business.

In many parts of the state, taverns were meeting places for the patriotically inclined men, as well as for the numerous people who adhered to the king and British crown. New Jersey had rightly been called "the cockpit of the Revolution." For several years the bulk of the fighting was done within her borders and the Continental Army spent three winters in camp here, two at Morristown and one at Middlebrook. Another winter was spent at Valley Forge in neighboring Pennsylvania.

Military roads were charted and taverns flourished along most of them. Later came the post roads and turnpikes. The inns, taverns, and just plain public houses really entered a heyday. The traffic generated by the York Road and other routes for the stagecoach lines that crisscrossed the state in all directions resulted in shelter for both man and beast at every crossroads and frequently far out in the country between places.

By the 1800s, public houses had grown up all around the state. Returning veterans, in particular men who had served in the Revolution, now sought licenses to open taverns. The age of so-called Washington Houses had arrived, and every village had its place where the commander-in-chief of the Continental Army set up his headquarters, or at least tarried for a while. I do not recall that I ever heard where the phrase originated, but I am certain that New Jersey was not remiss in saying that "Washington slept here."

Starting first in the northern part of the state, I have traveled everywhere in New Jersey to view the taverns that still exist from the Revolution. Many of them are from the colonial period, particularly in the southern part of the state, where changes have not taken place at so fast a pace. Others opened for business during or after the Revolution, apparently as the business demanded, but still in the latter part of the eighteenth century.

The first part of the nineteenth century and the so-called stagecoach era brought the tavern to a high tide in New Jersey. Nowadays the end not only of stage lines but of the railroads that came later, and the influence of the airplane on travel, have meant the abandoning of all but a handful of the old taverns. Those remaining in business have been modernized and cater to the ever-growing motor traffic with restaurant and dining facilities. They are on main highways, for the most part.

There is practically nothing left of the taverns that at one time strung along the Old Mine Road and, in fact, the ancient highway itself has largely disappeared, or has been absorbed into later and more modern thoroughfares. I traveled the length of it, from Kingston-on-the-Hudson to the point where it enters the northern reaches of Sussex County, in New Jersey, and on to Pahaquarry, near the Delaware, without finding any but modern taverns and dining places without claim to the past.

I have stood on a rock beside a low marker indicating that it is the corner where New Jersey, New York, and Pennsylvania come together. Above it a stone stated that it was the "Witness Monument 1882."

Montague and Brick House

At Montague the Brick House built in 1776 by Roger Clark stood until 1956. At one time it was noted as a stopping place for the New York to Oswego (N.Y.) stage, and during the Revolution it was a rallying point for patriots in the area. The old stage-line route from Montague to Deckertown and on to Jersey City ran directly past the Brick House, built of odd-size bricks that were said to have been made within a scant mile. I have told previously how the old inn was moved from its original site to make way for a traffic circle, and how it was finally demolished in the mid-1950s.

Wallpack Township

The old Van Campen House, a survivor of the Revolution, still stands in Wallpack Township, on the road to Dingman's Ferry. As an inn it provided shelter for John Adams and other famous persons on their way from New England to sessions of the Continental Congress in Philadelphia. An iron fireback still in the house when I last visited it was made at the nearby Oxford Furnace and was dated 1742.

Flatbrookville

Flatbrookville, founded in 1738 and survivor of the Revolution, still maintains a hotel of sorts. Some sixty years ago, when I first visited the place, it was a thriving community of about 700 souls, with stores, a lumberyard, mill, and hotel.

The first mail route from Flatbrookville to Newton was established in 1852, it is said.

Dropping southward we come next to the old York Road from Elizabethtown to Coryll's Ferry (Lambertville) enroute to Philadelphia. During the Revolution it was useful mainly as a military highway. Its prime purpose as a stagecoach line was served principally in the closing years of the eighteenth century and on into the next, until competition from railroads crossing the state ended the supremacy of travel by stage to and from New York and Philadelphia and places in between.

Elizabeth

In 1789 General Washington stopped in Elizabeth at the Red Lion Inn, which stood at South Broad Street and Rahway (St. George) Avenue. He was on the way from his home in Mount Vernon to New York to be inaugurated as the first president of the United States. Met by a delegation of leading citizens of the town, he was escorted to the inn. The procession was headed by General Mathias as grand marshal, and a reception at the inn was followed later by a luncheon at Boudinot Hall, on nearby East Jersey Street. After that, the procession continued down East Jersey Street to the waterfront on Staten Island Sound, where Washington took an eight-oar barge for the final part of his trip across the bay and around the Battery to the landing at the foot of Wall Street, and so to Federal Hall at Wall and Broad Streets in New York City, where he took the oath of office. The foregoing account is taken from the *New Jersey Journal* (now the Elizabeth *Daily Journal*), which was then published in Elizabethtown.

After the Revolution the inn was operated for a time as the Indian Queen and later on it was again called the Red

Lion Inn. It finally was torn down around the turn of the last century. Then the property was acquired by the city as site for the Public Library, which is still standing.

A long one-and-a-half-story building on South Broad Street, near the bridge over the Elizabeth River, was erected as early as 1728. During the Revolution it was a resort for British officers and their Tory friends, and was a special gathering place of the British military when they occupied the town. Around 1795 it was replaced by a stone building promptly named the Carteret Arms. After temporary success as a tavern, it was later occupied by the Elizabeth Orphan Asylum and, much later, by the Elizabeth Free Public Library, until 1913, when it first occupied the building erected for it on the old site of the Red Lion Inn.

Elizabethtown was the scene of much activity in the early years of the Revolution. British forces and Tories were encamped on Staten Island just across the Sound and later moved over to occupy the entire town. It was while Domine James Caldwell was debarking from a ship tied up at the Elizabethtown landing that he was shot by a sentry, who was finally tried in neighboring West Fields (Westfield) and then hanged at Gallows Hill in what is now East Broad Street. Caldwell's widow was shot later and killed by a British soldier's musket through a window at her home in Connecticut Farms (Union Township).

Newark

When Washington rode into Newark and down Broad Street on June 25, 1775, enroute to Boston and the command of the American troops, he tarried briefly for refreshments at the Eagle Tavern. Mr. MacWhorter, pastor of Newark's First Presbyterian Church since 1759, greeted him at the head of the local citizenry.

Late the following November, when Washington and his bedraggled army were in retreat across New Jersey after their defeat on Long Island, the American commander led 3,500 of his men into town and along Broad Street again. While his troops camped in the northern and western parts of Newark, Washington is reported to have made his headquarters at the Eagle Tavern. He stayed for nearly a week until activity on the part of the British obliged him, on November 28, 1775, to resume the retreat to the Delaware. His men left via the southern part of town as the enemy entered the northern reaches.

The Hounds and Horn Tavern on Broad Street was one of Newark's famed hostelries after the Revolution and on into the nineteenth century. Stages rattled into town over the Passaic River bridge and a short distance west into Broad Street and so to the establishment kept by the genial Amos Gifford at the corner of Market Street. Passengers alighted under the tavern sign depicting the end of a fox hunt, from whence came the name.

Everyone liked Gifford. His reputation for setting a fine table became legend, locally and among travelers. As he became better known, he also became something of a politician. It is no wonder, then, that he was appointed the first collector of customs when Newark was declared a port of entry in the country's history.

In 1800 an advertisement in Newark's only paper at the time, and also appearing in the *New Jersey Journal* published in nearby Elizabethtown, cited Gifford as offering to pay six cents apiece for quail to add to his menu at the tavern. His tavern became the best known in town and news of any importance was likely to be heard or repeated there. In 1804 the Newark & Essex Bank was organized at Gifford's Tavern by leading citizens of the town, who met there frequently to discuss problems of the day.

Although The Hounds and Horn, also known as Gifford's Tavern, was Newark's most popular gathering place of the time, there were others in the early 1800s. One such place was Seabury's Inn, a short way from Gifford's. Although the final organizing of the Newark & Essex Bank was at the latter's place in May 1804, it followed previous gatherings of local financiers at Seabury's to discuss the plan.

Captain Parkhurst, founder of a school bearing his name and otherwise a leader in local affairs, operated an inn on the west side of Broad Street, a few doors from Market Street, called The Rising Sun Tavern. It too was prominent in the early 1800s and served both food and drink. It was patronized both by the local citizenry and by passengers on stagecoaches from Paulus Hook right after they crossed the bridge over the Passaic River. Then there were Stephen and Moses Roff, each of whom conducted a tavern on Broad Street. Court was held at both places and at the time of local elections they were used as polling places. Across the street from the establishment of Moses Roff was a tavern known locally as Halsey's; early diaries tell of business conducted between the two places.

As the importance of Newark increased and the influx of people from Europe swelled in the nineteenth century, inns and then taverns became common. At one time five large breweries were located in Newark and specialized in setting up "saloons on every corner." Frequently each of the four corners at a street intersection had a competing tavern.

Later, the corner saloon in Newark and other cities across the state became ward or community rallying places. The proprietors were pillars of strength in politics. Frequently they were able to swing elections for their candidate for alderman, freeholder, and even state office. Then came the day when state law required that all "bars, café and other places dispensing intoxicating drink" close when voting polls were open. That law was not rescinded until 1971, and now it is a matter of local option.

The Morris Turnpike leads directly from Elizabeth to Springfield, Chatham, and Morristown, as it did in Revolutionary days. Enroute we pass through a town now called Madison, after the American president of that name. During the Revolution the section was known as Bottle Hill and the old Bottle Hill Tavern stands on the broad street to prove it. Now maintained as an eating place, the tavern was moved in 1923 from its original site further west on the same thoroughfare, at which time it was to be the home of the Madison Historical Society.

Morristown

Going on to Morristown, we come to the Dickerson Tavern of Revolutionary fame, at which time it was kept by a Robert Norris. It was in the westerly end of the taproom that the first trial of Benedict Arnold was held. The tavern is also linked with the courtship of Betsey Schuyler and Alexander Hamilton. They are said to have met secretly many times at the tavern when she was visiting an aunt just around the corner and he, in 1780, was an aide on the staff of General Washington.

The Widow White's Tavern, which stood "at the top of the hill" on present South Finlay Avenue of Basking Ridge, in the general Morristown area, had a direct and somewhat startling connection with the Revolution. It was there, on December 13, 1776, that a squadron of British dragoons from Staten Island captured General Charles Lee, second in command to Washington.

Surprised by the troopers when he was still in dressing gown, engaged in shaving while discussing morning events

Norris Tavern at Morristown, dating from 1763. Demolished in 1971. Benedict Arnold's court martial was held in the taproom. COURTESY THE NEW JERSEY HISTORICAL SOCIETY.

with aides, he was hastily mounted on a horse and ridden off, surrounded by the gleeful British captors. He was later exchanged for prisoners held by the Americans.

White's Tavern is sometimes referred to as Brewster's Tavern, according to a charmingly told story in a history of Basking Ridge prepared by the town's historical society for the statewide bicentennial celebration in 1964. The history, in a well-prepared pamphlet, also discusses villages in Basking Ridge Township, such as Liberty Corner and its "temperance tavern," Far Hills, and Veal Town (Bernardsville) with its stone hotel dating back to 1849.

An old map dating from 1781 in Princeton University's Firestone Library traces the route from Whippany, four miles north of Morristown, to Bullion's Tavern (Liberty Corner). It was drawn by Louis Alexander Berthier, who traveled with the French troops enroute to Yorktown as new allies in the American cause. Nothing further is known of Bullion's Tavern or its location.

Bedminster

A scant mile west of Far Hills, referred to above, is the lately refurbished Bedminster Inn, on the main street of the delightful old town of the same name. It has been a well-known hostelry in northern Somerset County for nearly two hundred years. Built originally in the 1780s, it is prominently mentioned in Andrew J. Mellick's classic "Story of an Old Farm," printed in 1898 in nearby Somerville by *The Messenger*, a newspaper. It is referred to by him as a center for farm folks in the area, as well as a stagecoach stop for travelers between Phillipsburg, Easton, and points along Delaware, and Elizabethtown, Newark, New York, and places in between.

During the late years of the last century the Bedminster Inn was a favorite summer place for New Yorkers and others seeking the country air and refuge from the summer heat. Its coach wagons and carriages met all trains at the nearby Far Hills station on the Morris & Essex branch of the DL&W Railroad. Two of the coaches are now preserved in the old barns at Sturbridge in western Massachusetts. Imagine my surprise on a recent trip to that place when I saw the familiar "Bedminster Inn, Bedminster, N.J." in gold lettering along the mid-section of each side of the vehicles!

There have been numerous proprietors of the Bedminster Inn over the years. Standing at the head of what was once Route 31 leading north from Somerville, it is bypassed by a spur of modern Route 206. Known for the last several years as the Cock & Bull, it is now operated as both tavern and restaurant, but it remains one of the few authentic public houses from the colonial era.

The inn dates from 1786, when it was built by John Aaron Mellick for his son, John, a former soldier in the Continental Army. The younger John and his bride, the former Jane Corriell, operated the inn until 1800, when it was sold to another

Bedminster Inn at Bedminster. The main section dates from 1780, and was built by John Aaron Mellick for his son, John, a Revolutionary War veteran.

Revolutionary veteran, Captain William Fulkerson. In 1825 it was owned by Peter Blair of Larger Crossroads. The next proprietors were Agatha and Dudwick Jefkin. They sold it in 1898 to Bertha and William Howard, in whose family it remained until 1963.

Much changed in recent years by successive renovations, the old tavern got much of its tradition from the long years of Howard ownership. It survived the prohibition days of the 1920s. Previously Woodrow Wilson, then head of Princeton University at Princeton, had made use of the front steps to address the assembled farm folks when he was running for governor of New Jersey.

Pottersville

I hope that my readers will pardon a short side trip over the rolling hills to Pottersville. It was the birthplace of my wife, the former Naomi Fritts, whom I married more than fifty years ago. I have referred in an earlier chapter to long-vanished taverns of the colonial era in the village.

The dates of the building and original opening of the old Pottersville Hotel are lost in the passing years. Most of the old residents in the quaint country hamlet of 300 souls, in the hills of northern Somerset county, agree that these events coincided with the laying of tracks for the Rockaway Railroad (Rockabye Line) from Whitehouse to Morristown early in the twentieth century.

Operated by a man named Sutton, the hotel was at one time a favorite weekend and summer gathering place for city folks, who came by stage to Morristown and then by train out to Pottersville station just behind the hotel. Standing back under great trees next to the village church graveyard, the hotel now houses a real estate office and dog-grooming shop on the ground floor. The onetime freight station now functions as a shed in a resident's backyard.

"I remember," says one old timer, "when the railroad shut down. The Government fellas came along and bought it up—track, train, engine and all. They shipped it to France and built a railroad there."

That was about 1915. The village is four miles away from Gladstone, where the branch line of the DL&W Railroad ends its run. In the last fifty years even the wooden ties of the railroad track have pretty much disappeared and the right of way across fields and streams is grown over with trees.

Pottersville was settled prior to the Revolution, and the first mill erected by William Willet is said to have ground corn and flour for Washington's army in winter quarters at Morristown. In the middle of the village the Black River helps form the junction of Somerset, Hunterdon, and Morris Counties. Across the valley there is a breathtaking view of Lamington Falls, which once provided water power for Pottersville's vanished industries. The ancient general store and tavern across from the sadly delapidated fulling mill was once a gathering place for farmers from miles around. They shopped and drank the famed "Jersey lightning" (hard apple cider) while waiting for their wheat and corn to be ground. The wheat flour was packed in sacks and marketed under the brand name "Hello My Lady." All trace of the early tavern keepers has been lost.

Watchung

Dropping south a few miles, we come to the Watchung Mountains and the rock promontory where Washington, his troops in winter camp at Jocky Hollow (Morristown) during the Revolution, kept an eye on the British in Elizabethtown and on Staten Island. On a clear day he could even see the British ships in New York harbor.

Along the road leading from Watchung into Plainfield was the Washington House. Kept by numerous proprietors since opening in the late 1700s as one of the first taverns to adopt the name of the commander in the Revolution, it nestled under a hill just off the road, and for years catered successively to the carriage and motor trade until totally destroyed by fire in the late 1950s.

Now we go back to Elizabethtown Point, where the Old York Road got its start in 1764 as a through route from New York clear across the state to the Delaware and so on to Philadelphia. The road had been in use for more than a decade when the Revolution broke out, and military forces

Washington House signpost at Basking Ridge, probably 18th century. Photographed in 1950, it is now gone.

on both sides were quick to realize its value. After the first few months civilian traffic and freight ended because stage lines and feeder short lines discontinued for the duration, and the movement of troops and their supplies became practically the sole function of the road.

Undoubtedly there were inns and plain taverns, holdovers from colonial days, at the Elizabethtown Point end of the Old York Road during the Revolution and even afterward. If so, they have vanished, and even tradition seems to have forgotten them. As a matter of fact, the first trace of a public house along the Old York Road is the inn at Scotch Plains.

Scotch Plains

The names of early landlords of the old inn at the corner of Park Avenue and East Front Street are lost with the passing of time. There is a permanent record among old Essex County deeds, however, showing that "on January 8, 1788, David Morris and his wife, Mary, of Elizabethtown, in the County of Essex, convey to Recompense Stanbury, Tavern-keeper of the same place, a piece of land beginning at a stake standing in the line of Joseph Searing's land bounded by Jacob Frazee's land."

Records of the Scotch Plains Baptist Church show that David Morris subsequently moved to Kentucky, as did a number of the village's other Revolutionary War veterans.

In the *New Jersey Journal* (Elizabethtown) for May 21, 1791, the following notice appeared:

> By John Chetwood, Esq., one of the Justices of the Supreme Court of New Jersey—Notice is hereby given that on application to me by Thomas Frazer (Frazee), his wife, Hannah Searing, one of the daughters of Joseph Searing, dec. and which said Hannah Searing claims as an undivided third in such property—at a place called Scotch Plains—said property adjoining the lands of Joseph

Hutchins, Melvin Pierce & Anthony Littell—also adjoins lands of Jacob Stanbury, William Darby and Recompense Stanbury, Inn-keeper at the Scotch Plains.

Another notice in the same newspaper on March 16, 1818, states that "Nathan Squire, Sheriff, will sell on that date certain mortgaged premises, between the hours of 12 and 5 in the afternoon, in the house of Jacob Stanbury, Inn-keeper." The land referred to is directly across from the Stage House Inn and after the date mentioned it was the site of a dwelling occupied for many years by the family and descendants of John R. Marsh, one of the village's early settlers.

I remember as a small boy that the Marsh house was taken over in the early 1900s by Henry C. Meyer, who kept the general store across the street at Park and Bartle Avenues. When Meyer died it was taken over by Alexander Muir, who had married Marion, one of Meyer's daughters. The house was torn down by the town in 1945 and the land is now the site of the town hall. Next door to the land, on the East Front Street side, is the so-called Cannonball House, now owned by the township and home of the recently organized Scotch Plains-Fanwood Historical Society. The house is said to have cannonballs embedded in its walls from the fighting between Continental and British troops during the Revolution.

Jacob Stanbury was the last of the family to operate the Stage House Inn. The Baptist Church records show that he died in 1821 and was buried in the adjoining graveyard. I recall as a youth his grandson, also named Recompense, who lived at Park Avenue and the Mountain Road leading to Springfield. The house has been moved to the rear of the lot facing on Park Avenue and is a rooming house for Filipinos working at a restaurant across the street. A gasoline filling station occupies the corner.

With the advent of the railroad from Elizabeth to Somerville, which originally ran along Midway Avenue, and the consequent loss of patronage at the Stage House Inn as a regular stop on the Swift Sure Stage Line, the tavern lost prestige and business fell on evil days. It was not aided by the organizing of a local temperance society in 1831, meeting "in early candlelight" in the schoolhouse (now occupied by the YMCA) on Stout Avenue.

According to a map drawn by Robert Erskene for use by the Continental forces and now in the New York Historical Society collections, the old tavern was kept during the Revolution by a landlord named Marselis. One of my boyhood recollections is of "Dummy" Deegan, a onetime pitcher for the New York Yankees, as innkeeper in the early 1900s. He was followed by Herman Frowery, and the field in the rear, now a parking lot, was laid out as a baseball diamond for the Scotch Plains All Stars. Later, the tavern served for a brief time as a teen-age center and then faced demolition before it was finally decided to modernize it for its present use as a restaurant.

Many weary travelers found refreshment for man and beast at the tavern and inn of Johnathan Osborne on East Front Street, which was known in earlier days as simply "the road to Plainfield." The first reference I have found to it is in a newspaper extract in the New Jersey Archives advertising in 1771 for "an inn-keeper at Scotch Plains, N.J."

Osborne's Tavern was midway between Park Avenue and Terrill Road, according to the map referred to above. Although it was on the original Old York Road, the lack of regular stagecoach stops relegated it to being patronized mostly by local men. It was known for years as the Halfway House after the last of the Osbornes left in the early 1800s. The original building was destroyed by fire in the 1940s and the site is now occupied by a one-story tavern of brick.

In 1775 Amos Swan was doing business in Swan's Tavern

on the old Mountain Road. According to a notice in the *New Jersey Journal*[1] the tavern was "at the plantation of Amos Swan, Scotch Plains, a short half mile from the meeting house, on the road to Springfield."

Also in the *New Jersey Journal* in 1780 Amos Swan had a notice that read:

"At the house of the subscriber at the Scotch Plains, seven miles from Springfield, on the road leading from thence to Princeton, horses bought, sold and traded." Swan dealt in horses as well as keeping an adjoining tavern. An old bill found among the papers of John Frazee, Central Avenue, Westfield, who died in February 1970 at age ninety-eight, shows the following:

David Squires to Amos Swan, Dr;

1775 April to Sundry	0.4.11
1777 July 29 To Rum & Ldg.	0.3.9.
1781 Jan 18 For Grogg	6.1.0 &
	6.9.8
To interest on ye above	0.6.11
	0.16.7

The *New Jersey Journal* for March 8, 1780, carried the following:

"Notice is hereby given by Daniel Marsh, Quartermaster, Militia, to those having claims against his department—to meet him on Tuesday, March 11, at Swan's Tavern, Scotch Plains."

Records of the Scotch Plains Baptist Church show that Amos Swan died November 16, 1782.

My earliest recollections of the Scotch Plains–Fanwood area, where I have lived as boy and man since 1901, include Walpole's Hotel, at Park Avenue and Second Street. It was a

1. New Jersey Ext., 1778. New Jersey Archives, p. 158.

place I was warned by my parents never to enter. I managed, however, to witness a few of the cockfights held stealthily by lantern light on moonless nights in the enclosed courtyard in the rear.

When the hotel started, I do not know. The building still stands on the original site, although a confectionery and other stores have been erected in front of it along Park Avenue and the courtyard is gone. In place of the long porch that formerly extended along the front of the structure, there is a sidewalk. I recall that baseball games in the field diagonally across the street often ended in fighting augmented by the swinging of stout railings pulled from the porch.

Honeymoon couples from Stony Hill and the area along the Watchung Mountain often spent their wedding night in second-floor bedrooms at Walpole's Hotel. They seemed totally oblivious of the noise of the taproom below.

In my youth there was Guttridge's Tavern at Terrill Road and East Second Street, now occupied by the Jade Isle, a Chinese-American restaurant. There was also a small hotel, with bar and a few other rooms, out in the country at Raritan Road and Inman Avenue, in the so-called Willow Grove section of the township. The intersection was known as Dog Corners, because farmers for miles around gathered there on Saturday night. They talked of many things over the glass that cheers, while their faithful animals waited outside to see that they got safely home.

In recent times the old wooden-framed building was turned into a private residence, but it has now been torn down to make way for a housing development. When it was first started, or its landlords, is unknown to me.

Plainfield

My first employment was with the nearby *Plainfield Daily*

Press as a reporter. I soon became familiar with all the city's hotels and their history. During the Revolution Plainfield was but a very small village and did not have the standing even of Scotch Plains. Over the years it has increased in both population and importance, while Scotch Plains has actually lost ground.

Laing's Hotel was built on West Front Street, Plainfield, in 1828, shortly before the coming of the railroad and too late for most of the stagecoach lines on the Old York Road which it fronted. A favorite stop for travelers from the Watchung Hills country and theater companies, it was also a gathering place for local affairs. Integrated into the Babcock Building in 1893, it was destroyed by fire that gutted the larger structure in the late 1960s.

The ground floor was surrounded by the usual wide veranda that served as a shelter for passersby in snow and rain. In the early years it was a stopping place for stagecoaches running along the Old York Road to and from Paulus Hook, Newark, and Philadelphia.

It was in the 1860s that the hotel gained its greatest civic attraction, with numerous meetings held there in 1868 to discuss application to the legislature for a city charter. The charter was granted in April 1869, and a gala party at the hotel celebrated the event.

According to an item in the *Daily Press* for March 12, 1892, the hotel was to be sold at public auction the following March 21 to satisfy foreclosure of three mortgages. A later account indicates that it brought $28,275 over and above the mortgages.

Jacob Blimm built the Farmers' Hotel at Somerset and West Front Streets in the mid-1800s. It was long popular with farmers living in the Warren, Mt. Bethel, and Washington Valley areas. Folks for miles around would park their horses and wagons, carriages, or buggies in sheds behind the hotel while on shopping trips to town. Often the farmers brought eggs, butter, and other farm produce to sell at local stores. Sometimes they sought only refreshment and shelter. I last knew of the place as Gloeckner's Tavern. It was torn down in 1926 to make way for a dress shop and department store annex.

The Hotel Waldorf on East Front Street was run by Henry Windham, and it and its adjoining restaurant were busy places in downtown Plainfield at the turn of the century. The ninety-foot bar was famous throughout the central part of the state. Whiskey sold at ten cents a drink. Windham sold the building in 1918 and moved to the Hotel Iroquois at Park Avenue and Second Street. Later he changed the name to the Queen City Hotel and in 1920 sold out to Arthur Flourish. When the street was widened in 1925 and Flourish had moved into the new Park Hotel at West Seventh Street and Arlington Avenue, the Queen City Hotel was torn down to make room for a commercial structure.

From Plainfield the Old York Road takes us to Bound Brook, where the Fisher Tavern once stood near Middlebrook Creek, the town's western boundary. It was in nearby Camp Middlebrook that Washington, on July 4, 1777, is said to have first unfurled the thirteen-star flag made by Betsey Ross in Philadelphia.

At Bound Brook the Old York Road takes a sharp left turn off present-day Route 28, which comes from Plainfield. On Bound Brook's main street there is another left turn under the CNJ railroad tracks before we reach a stretch of the Old York Road between the tracks of the CNJ and the Lehigh Valley Railroad. Another sharp left turn takes us to an old stone bridge just west of where the Old York Road at one time had a junction with the King's Highway.

Somerville

Passing the Van Horn and Van Vechten houses on bluffs overlooking the Raritan River, we proceed toward Somerville, described in an 1825 issue of the Somerset *County Messenger* as "combining many advantages. It is central, healthy, pleasant and easy of access. The Swift Sure stage from New York to Philadelphia passes through three times a week, and a stage connecting with a line of stages and steamboats at New Brunswick, leaves the village every morning for that city and returns in the afternoon."

As we enter the town's main street, the Somerville Hotel stands on the right. It is said to contain some of the old Tunison Tavern, but changes were made long enough ago that the hotel itself enjoyed some of the traffic from stagecoach days along the Old York Road. Besides other landmarks, the town has the state-operated Wallace House, which was used by Washington as headquarters during the time the Continental Army was at Camp Middlebrook. There is also the Dutch Parsonage, built for the Rev. John Frelinghuysen in 1751, when he was pastor of churches in the Raritan Valley. Maintained by the DAR, it is the "cradle of Rutgers University."

Centerville

Proceeding west on the Old York Road through Raritan and Readington, we come next to Centerville. Modern Route 202 is crossed several times, and there is also the Duke Estate, made up of old farms that flourished during the stagecoach era. At Centerville the tavern at the crossroads has burned down and the original barn that sheltered horses in stagecoach days along the Old York Road is now a community center.

In *Two Hundred and Fifty Years of Old Somerset*, the late

Van Doren Honeyman states that "the blare of the coach horn can be heard a half-mile as the east or west bound coach approaches the village of Centerville."

Larison's Corner

Larison's Corner is the next stop on the Old York Road after passing through Three Bridges and Reaville, which retain much of their old flavor, but the days of the stage-coach are gone forever. Just across from the ancient cemetery is the site of Larison's Tavern, which catered to the local farmers for miles around and also to the early nineteenth-century stagecoach traffic on the Old York Road. At Reaville the Old York Road has a junction with the Amwell Road; still in use as the most direct way to New Brunswick.

Ringoes

Ringoes is only a few miles west of Larison's Corner. Until the early years of the nineteenth century, it was a main stop for stage lines on the Old York Road; then the route was shifted to Flemington. Ringoes was settled in 1721 and for years was the trading center of the entire Amwell Valley. Still standing on the Main Street, and now used on the ground floor as a liquor store, is the Amwell Academy building erected of native brick made in the vicinity. The remains of Peter Johan Rockefeller, the first of the family in this country, lie in the ancient graveyard at Ringoes. All trace of the first tavern, and of the later public house used by stage-coach passengers, is gone.

The route from Ringoes to Lambertville is much the same as it was in the time of the Old York Road. At Mount Airy, passed on the way, the old tavern that entertained travelers by stage still stands, although it is now a private dwelling.

White House

White House, ten miles north of Flemington and really off the Old York Road, had its share of travelers in stagecoach days, with traffic heavy on the Easton to New Brunswick Turnpike and various feeder lines. During the Revolution the tavern, kept by Abraham Van Horn and his son from 1760 until 1775, was the most popular hostelry for miles around. Located at the juncture of two branches of the Rockaway River on the road from Clinton to Somerville, it was ideally situated for business in the nineteenth century.

John Connel followed the junior Van Horn as landlord for a brief time and next was Aaron T. Lucas. During the latter's tenure, a court of inquiry held at the tavern by order of General Dickinson of Revolutionary fame found no cause for action against Colonel John Taylor, commanding the Fourth Regiment of Hunterdon County Militia. He was charged with cowardice in the face of the enemy. In April 1781, residents of the county "with claims against the Congress under requisitions by General Washington" were instructed to meet the accounting officer for the government at the White House Tavern, where he was staying.

The White House Tavern was rented in May 1781 by Cornelius Tunison, who is recorded as filing a protest with the Hunterdon Court the next year against the granting of a license for Captain Richard Stilwell to operate a tavern less than two hundred yards away. He continued on, however, until 1800, when license applications were signed by Cornelius W. Van Horn.

Captain Stilwell began operating his tavern, called the New White House, in 1783. He continued until 1792 and was followed by Daniel Cowenhoven for five years before Jesse Roberts became landlord, according to license applications.

Bethlehem

Another old public house in the area was the Hickory Tavern in what was once called Bethlehem, Sussex County. It was started prior to 1759, according to a "To be Lett or Sold" notice in the *Pennsylvania Gazette* for January 11 of that year, and continued under various landlords until it was discontinued in 1867. It was kept during the Revolution by Peter Howell and was the scene of many patriotic gatherings. In 1780 Spencer Carter, who had been landlord in 1760s, returned until 1796, according to renewal applications filed with the county court each year. Peter Van Syckle, who took over in that year, built a large frame house in 1800 to replace the previously used log cabin. He continued until 1830 and was succeeded by a son, who died after two years and was followed by several other innkeepers.

Clinton

Near Clinton the Boar's Head Tavern was kept during the Revolution by Abraham Bonnel, who died in 1797. At a meeting of citizens in the area held at the tavern late in 1775, a regiment of militia was organized. The commander was Charles Stewart, who was elected colonel. Other officers were Lieutenant Colonel Mark Tompson, and Majors Frederick Frelinghuysen and Thomas Henderson. The following February the regiment was ordered by the Provincial Congress of New Jersey to join the Continental forces then in New York City. That same year Bonnel was elected lieutenant colonel of the Second Regiment, Hunterdon County Militia. At one time he represented the community on the Board of Freeholders and was an early delegate to the Sons of Liberty organized at Ringo's Tavern in nearby Ringoes. Descendants in the Bonnel family were license applicants for many years.

The Jones Tavern was another Clinton public house during the Revolution. It was started before the war by Captain Thomas Jones, who kept it until his death in 1787. During the Revolution he was away checking on the Durham boats on the Delaware for Washington when a band of Tories in the neighborhood broke into the tavern and abused members of his family. On June 26, 1776, the Provincial Congress ordered the militia to arrest the culprits, but the outcome is not known.

In 1779 the properties of persons convicted in the county courts of disloyalty were ordered sold "at the house of Thomas Jones." After 1787 there was a succession of unidentified landlords of Jones Tavern.

New Hampton

At New Hampton, on the Musconetcong Creek, the Mackey Tavern was kept during the Revolution by Amos Swesey (Swayze), according to his application for a license dated in 1775. Sixty-odd years ago I knew a Justice Swayze from Somerville. He was a descendant, and a member of the New Jersey Supreme Court.

Jacob Johnson, Jr., is listed as tavern keeper from 1782 to 1785, and during the early years of the nineteenth century the landlords were members of the John Matlock family.

Along the Delaware from Lambertville south there were a number of taverns important during the Revolution and the stagecoach era. One such place was the Bear Tavern, at the intersection of the road from McKonkey's Ferry and the road to Pennington. Crossing the River Road, it is eight or nine miles from Trenton. Enroute to the Battle of Trenton, the entire Continental Army, after recrossing the Delaware, passed by the Bear Tavern.

Andrew Mershon is the first landlord of record at the tavern. Apparently he was the keeper during the Revolution until death sometime after 1792, when his will, on file with other old Hunterdon documents, is dated. Jesse Atchley was granted a license in 1800, and in 1813 the place was sold to John Huff. Next came John Hart, whose only license application on file is dated in 1818.

Flemington

Nathaniel Lowery was innkeeper of the Samuel Fleming Tavern, the first in Flemington, during the Revolution. It is now owned by the Colonel Lowery Chapter, DAR. Other taverns of the same period were those of Nathaniel Parker from 1774 to 1778 and George Alexander from 1775 to 1795, according to license renewal applications on file in the county court.

Stockton

Just off the main path to Lambertville and to the south is the village of Stockton. On the main street of the village is the Stockton Inn, a 140-year-old landmark of the Hunterdon County town bearing the same name. It has been used constantly ever since it was built in 1832 by Asher Johnson. It passed through several ownerships before it was acquired by Charles Colligan, whose grandson is the present innkeeper.

Until the 1940s it was headquarters for salesmen and peddlers who sold their wares up and down the Delaware River country nearby. Gas rationing during World War II put an end to that, and the renting of rooms was halted in favor of an enlarged dining room and bar. The inn now serves more meals over a summer weekend than it did in an entire year in the old days.

Stockton Inn, Stockton, in 1973. Established in 1832. COURTESY RICHARD M. LEA.

"Adela St. John, the writer, was staying at the inn in 1932," according to the present Colligan, "when she was visited by the song-writing team of Rogers and Hart. They took a room to complete work on the musical "On Your Toes." The Inn's wishing-well gave them the idea for the show's hit tune about a small hotel and its wishing well."

A few years later the inn was headquarters for newspaper

reporters covering the Bruno Hauptmann trial at Flemington, a scant ten miles away, where the German-born carpenter was found guilty of kidnapping the baby of the Charles Lindberghs and later was hanged.

In the early 1700s, Stockton was known as Reading, after an original settler. Later it was called Howell's Ferry after a Joseph Howell, operator of a ferry across the Delaware River. Then it became known as Center Bridge and, finally, in 1851, when a post office was set up, it was named after Richard Stockton, Jersey patriot and signer of the Declaration of Independence.

The town's 600-odd residents are mostly a close-knit lot. There are few changes, and a stranger in their midst is a novelty.

Lambertville

Lambertville, on the Delaware, marks the end of the Old York Road in New Jersey. Known long ago as Coryll's Ferry, the crossing of the river is now by bridge to New Hope and other towns on the Old York Road in Pennsylvania. On the main street of the town is the Lambertville House, built in 1812, by Captain John Lambert on the site of an earlier stone tavern. Patronized now mainly by motoring diners attracted by the quaint serenity of the place and its good food, the inn also accommodates overnight guests just as it took care of travelers in the stagecoach days on the Old York Road.

On Bridge Street is the house in which James Wilson Marshall was born in 1810. A carpenter's son, he later worked his way by degrees to California and in 1848, while helping to build a sawmill on the American River, he first discovered gold with his partner, General John Sutter, but both men were without funds when they died.

Lambertville Inn, Lambertville, in 1973. Established in 1812. COURTESY RICHARD M. LEA.

In the graveyard of the nearby Presbyterian Church lie the remains of George Coryll, son of the village's founder. The son died at age ninety-two on February 18, 1851, according to the tombstone inscription.

In his *History of Hunterdon and Somerset Counties* printed in 1880, James P. Snell has this to say of Lambertville:

The hills immediately to the east and southeast of the town are quite bold and abrupt, but those to the north and northeast rise up with gentle activity. From these hills there are extensive and beautiful views of the surrounding country. Few places have more picturesque surroundings than has Lambertville, and the wonder is that it has not attracted more of the attention of lovers of fine scenery.

Rahway

All trace of the old taverns on present-day St. George Avenue, known first as the King's Highway, and the road to Bridgetown (later Quibbletown and finally Rahway) is gone, through Elizabeth (Elizabethtown), until we reach the Merchants and Drovers Tavern still standing on the outskirts of Rahway at the intersection of St. George Avenue and the road to Westfield. It was a stopping place on the stage line of John Mercereau and John Barnhill, who made bi-weekly trips from Paulus Hook to Philadelphia, according to a broadside from 1776 in the New York Historical Society. After the Revolution it came into the possession of Dr. David Stuart Craig, a leading Rahway physician of the time, through his marriage to Phoebe, a daughter of John Anderson, the first licensee of record.

The Wheat Sheaf Inn and other taverns of the Revolutionary era that I remember as a boy in the early 1900s, when St. George Avenue still ran through open country from Elizabeth to Rahway and beyond to New Brunswick, are all gone in the face of progress.

At Woodbridge there was a tavern called the Cross and Key that played an important role during the Revolution. Besides sheltering numerous important travelers of those years, it was at the junction of the Kings Highway with Lawries' Road, which started at Imlaytown and Allentown in South Jersey. Couriers and officers made the tavern a stopping place. All traces of the tavern and its landlords have been lost.

New Brunswick

The Indian Queen Tavern in New Brunswick has been dealt with quite fully in an earlier chapter. I have encountered the same name at least two other times in my wanderings around the state. After the Revolution and presumably under new ownership, it was known as the Colonial American Hotel, apparently to denote its ancient origin. It was demolished in the mid-1960s. During the Revolution it was a stopping place for Franklin, Adams, and Rutledge when on their way to a conference with Lord Howe on Staten Island over prisoners of war and possible peace.

The Whitehall Tavern, originally started back in 1756, according to Walter Lester Glenney's *Historic Roadsides of New Jersey* published in 1928, was another prominent stagecoach stop during the Revolution and after into the nineteenth century.

After crossing the Raritan at New Brunswick, the King's Highway passed through open country in Revolutionary times and later, into the nineteenth century, until it reached Kingston. During the final days of the Revolution, when the Continental Congress sat at Princeton and Washington occupied the Berrien House at Rocky Hill, a spur was constructed off the main road for the convenience of travelers to meet with Washington at Rocky Hill. Tradition has it that the courier bringing word of the treaty-signing at Ghent, Belgium, that ended the war landed from a ship at New Brunswick, from whence he rode horseback over the King's Highway and detoured to find Washington at Rocky Hill.

Rocky Hill

Washington stayed at Rocky Hill from August 24 to November 10, 1783, four miles from Princeton, while the

Continental Congress, driven from Philadelphia, met in Nassau Hall of Princeton University. While there, he is said to have written his farewell address later delivered to his officers assembled at Fraunce's Tavern, in lower New York. He read it for the first time to members of his bodyguard standing on the lawn at the rear of the Berrien mansion, where he maintained headquarters. The Berrien house was moved in later years to a location further up the hill so that traprock mining operations would not be impeded.

Princeton

At Princeton the time of the Revolution and years thereafter were stirring times. The King's Highway, the most direct path between New York and Philadelphia, ran along its main street, and the taverns on it were filled constantly with members of Congress and others prominent in their day. After the so-called Battle of Princeton on January 3, 1777, Washington led his army north into winter quarters at Morristown. The four boulders, with bronze tablets erected by the DAR to mark sections of the route he took, are at Griggstown; on the Court House grounds at Somerville; at the old Allen Tavern on Route 31 (now 206); and at Kenilworth Inn on the outskirts of Pluckemin.

Jacob G. Bergen was landlord of the tavern at the Sign of the New Jersey College on Princeton's main street during the Revolution. The state's Legislature and Council of Safety held frequent meetings there, as evidenced by minutes of the Assembly authorizing payment of various sums for rooms and food. Christopher Beekman took over in 1779 and remained until 1787, when he moved to Washington Inn, the location of which is not indicated on his license application.

During Beekman's tenure, Independence Day was celebrated at Princeton on July 4, 1781, with the Governor and other important personages present. Without stating where the celebration was held, histories of the town say that the people honored later repaired to the tavern at the Sign of the New Jersey College for refreshments and good fellowship. Another occasion celebrated at the Beekman tavern was the surrender of Cornwallis at Yorktown on October 3, 1781.

David Goodwin was proprietor of the tavern at the Sign of the New Jersey College from 1787 until 1799, when John Gifford, son of Arthur Gifford, genial landlord of Newark fame, took over. He lasted until 1812 and was followed by John Joline until 1835. It was during Joline's years that the tavern became known for the first time as Nassau Inn, a name it holds to this day.

The tavern at the Sign of the Hudibras, at the corner of College Lane and the main street in Princeton, was kept during the Revolution by Jacob Hyer. On October 7, 1782, he filed with Congress a claim for outrages committed by the British. He was a patriot and lieutenant colonel of the Third Regiment, Middlesex County Militia, when it was formed in1776, but after two years he resigned in December 1778.

Officers from Morristown and places to the north on the way to Philadelphia, where Congress was meeting, always stopped at the Hyer tavern, and later, when Congress met in Nassau Hall in 1783, a courier of messages and documents to Washington at Rocky Hill stayed there.

Hyer was succeeded in 1804 by Jacob C. Ten Eyck, with John Joline following in 1810. After two years at the Hudibras tavern, Ten Eyck was succeeded in 1812 by George Follet. Next came Zebulon Morford, who was followed in 1826 by Joseph J. Thompson, under whose tenure the old building was greatly improved and renamed the City Hotel. The building was finally demolished in the 1870s to permit expansion of the Princeton University campus.

For a short time after leaving the Sign of the New Jersey

College in 1787, Christopher Beekman apparently went over to the Washington Inn, also on Nassau Street, which was the village's main thoroughfare then as it is at the present time. In 1804, the record shows, the inn was acquired by a member of the Stryker family and apparently it stayed in their possession for many years. Previously it was kept for brief periods by six different landlords, as is indicated by license applications filed with the court.

Other taverns in Princeton during the Revolution and later were the King's Arms and the Thirteen Stars, later changed to the Sign of the Confederation.

Trenton

There were at least a dozen taverns in Trenton during and after the Revolution. I have listed previously those of colonial origin. Isaiah Yard, grandson of the first innkeeper, reopened the Yard Tavern in Front Street in 1780, following a five-year closing brought on by the war and British occupation. In 1783, when he first petitioned for a license, he stated that he had taken "the Noted Tavern known by the Name of Yard's Tavern in the Lower Street in Trenton aforesed in which said place has been a Tavern kept from the first settlement of said town till within these few years past."

The Ship & Castle Tavern on Front Street, alongside the Yard Tavern, was kept in 1774 by Joseph Clunn, according to his license application filed with the court on May 2 of that year. It was closed in 1776 by the war.

During the Revolution, the Black Horse Tavern, sometimes known as the Royal Oaks, kept going, apparently in large part because of the Tory affiliations of its landlords. From 1773 to 1778, for instance, Rachel Stille, a widow, was landlord. She was a sister of John Barnes, who was sheriff of

Hunterdon County when war broke out. He resigned the post and joined the First Battalion of New Jersey Volunteers as a major. He was killed during a skirmish in which the Loyalist organization took part on Staten Island in 1777, the record shows. In 1778 the place was sold to Joseph Miller and then rented to a Captain John Yard, who appears to have been the innkeeper until 1782. Its site at the corner of State and Broad Streets is now used for commercial purposes.

The King of Prussia Tavern, at the upper end of present-day Warren Street, was kept until 1776 by Charles Axford, who was paid money on October 5, 1775, by order of the Continental Congress for "provisions furnished Captain James Ross' riflemen who passed through Trenton on the way to Cambridge." In December 1781, he filed claim for damages sustained from Continental troops.

The Indian King Tavern on Warren Street near East Hanover Street, was kept by Charity Britten during the Revolution until July 31, 1779. On that date Isaac Britten announced that he had "settled himself in his owne House lately and long Occupied by Mrs. Charity Britten as a Tavern." Whether he was a son or other kin is not stated. In 1784 Joseph Smith announced that he had "rented that Ancient Stand formerly Known by the Name of the Indian King in Trenton aforesaid with the Intention of Keeping a Publick House of Entertainment." Later the same year John Polhemus applied to the court for permission to keep "a public house in the house of the Late Isaac Britten in Trenton." James McKinlay reported in 1791 that he had gone to "considerable expence fitting up and furnishing the well known House formerly occupied by Mrs. Britten and Others." Apparently he remained until 1808, when Benjamin Fish sought a license and stated that the tavern was "the starting point for stage coaches between Trenton-Philadelphia."

The name was changed to the Union Tavern when John

Howell and Abner Scudder took over in 1817. William J. Leslie, a clockmaker formerly in Freehold, and one of whose tall clocks, with a labeled case by Mathew Egerton, New Brunswick craftsman, is now in the Monmouth County Historical Society building at Freehold, advertised in 1805 that he was doing business in a store "located between the Indian King Tavern and the Union Hotel."

The Indian Queen Tavern, also on Warren street, on the site recently occupied by the Trent Theater, was closed during the war and did not reopen until 1798, when James B. Cooper sought a license. He called it the Native American Tavern, according to his first application. During his time Washington's Birthday was celebrated at the Indian Queen Tavern. An item in the Trenton *Federalist* for March 4, 1799, has an elaborate account of the "brilliant ball given by subscription of the citizens at James B. Cooper's inn."

John Anderson took over in May 1800, according to announcement in the *Federalist* that he had "moved from the City Hotel to the Indian Queen Tavern." A year later he was succeeded by Peter Probasco. In 1819 the tavern was offered for sale. At that time it was reported as "part of the estate of Andrew Blackwell, dec'ed." After having five or six subsequent landlords, the Indian Queen Tavern was bought by Samuel Kay in 1847 and the name was changed to the United States Hotel.

Still's Tavern at Warren and Perry streets has been mentioned previously as one of Trenton's colonial public houses. After Pontius Still had sold it, the tavern was an active place during the Revolution, although the name of the proprietor has not been established. When the British occupied Trenton in December 1776, and during the American attack on Christmas Eve of that year, it was headquarters and guardhouse for the Hessian detachment under Colonel Rahl.

Other taverns in Trenton during and after the Revolution

included the Green Tree Inn, the Blazing Star Tavern, the City Hotel, the Sign of the Fox Tavern, and the New Jersey Dragoon Tavern. All of them played a part during the war and later when the state government was set up in Trenton.

Perth Amboy

At Perth Amboy, on the banks of the Raritan, just before the King's Highway branched off toward Imlaytown and Allentown, there were a number of old taverns to shelter travelers. In colonial times this was an important seaport. Its taverns entertained many immigrants overnight before they continued to their destination, including the band of Scots who founded Scotch Plains and numerous others.

During World War I the Gillespie Shell Loading Company plant at nearby Morgan blew up. I crossed the long railroad trestle over the Raritan several times on foot, seeking a telephone in the deserted Packer House in New Brunswick, to let the world know the horrifying word through the pages of New York newspapers. I was in newspaper work at the time as a reporter.

During the pioneer days of automobiling and trips to the Jersey shore, the "hole in the wall" tunneled under the Pennsylvania Railroad embankment allowed only a single line of traffic at a time. It was early in the present century and roads were very different from what they are today. Weary motorists returning from the shore were delayed for hours in reaching home and traffic backed up several miles waiting for southbound vehicles to pass.

Much of today's traffic passes above Perth Amboy on high bridges without ever seeing, much less stopping in, the ancient city. The public houses of Revolutionary days are in the past, identifiable only by memorial markers on the site.

Bordentown

After leaving Trenton, the first town of size during the Revolution was Bordentown, where there were at least five taverns of that vintage. One of them was originally started in colonial times by Dr. Joseph Brown, a son-in-law of Col. Joseph Borden, after whom the town is named. It was kept by George Applegate from 1761 until his death in 1812, except for the single year 1808, when David Fenimore applied for the license, according to court records. During the Revolution he first sought and was granted British immunity when troops under Lord Howe took possession of the town, but later recanted to the Council of Safety. In 1780 he filed claim with the New Jersey Legislature meeting at Burlington, for losses to the British in the total amount of 164.14.6 for the years 1776, 1778, and 1779.

After Applegate's death his widow, Deborah, was tavern keeper for four years, then she was succeeded by Joshua Carman. During Applegate's tenure it became the style to call public houses after the wartime commander and he accordingly renamed his place the Washington House. The new name appears in court records after 1790.

Oakey Hoagland kept the American House at present-day Park and Farnesworth Avenues from 1774 through 1787, according to court records. During the war he was a major in the First Regiment, Burlington County Militia, and at one time the New Jersey Legislature, then at Trenton, put him in charge of all ferries along the Delaware "to keep out undesirables. " After the capture of Lieutenant Colonel James G. Simcoe in October 1779, following the famed Simcoe raid, the British officer was billeted at Hoagland's tavern during his parole.

The claim book now on file in the New Jersey State

Library at Trenton records that Hoagland filed claim for a total of 82.3.6 damage incurred during British occupancy of Bordentown, but the claim is not marked paid by the New Jersey Legislature. In 1883 citizens of the town met at Hoagland's tavern to mark the ending of the war. Hoagland moved to Burlington in 1787.

During the winter of 1775-76 a group of "literary lights," meeting as a club in Matthew Potter's tavern in Bridgeton, posted a series of eight weekly essays alongside the great fireplace in the taproom of the tavern. The site of the tavern was at present-day 49 and 51 Broad Street. According to the late Charles S. Boyer, the tavern was kept from 1753 to 1770 by Joseph Bishop.

In the early part of 1773, according to Boyer, the next proprietor was Matthew Potter, Jr., who had erected a new house on the site of the former Bishop tavern. He was licensed to operate the place from 1774 to 1779, and it became a favorite meeting place for the young men of the neighborhood. Young Potter, a brother of Colonel David Potter, had removed from Philadelphia, where he sold his holdings in March 1773.

The club's essays were written in the style of the day. The contributors included Joseph Bloomfield and Richard Howell, both of whom later became governors of New Jersey. Only one copy of each of the eight issues is known to exist. The paper is said to have been the pioneer of all others in Cumberland County. Dr. Jonathan Elmer was president of the group sponsoring it, and Ebenezer Elmer was the secretary.

Potter remained at the tavern until 1782, except for 1777, when it was kept by Simon Souder, according to Boyer. Early deeds describe the site as "on the north side of the main street near the Court House, on the brow of the Hill." Daniel Mulford was keeping the Potter tavern from 1782 to

1785. Thereafter, until its demolition, it was occupied by a cobbler named John Sibley.

Freehold

Probably the oldest tavern in Freehold, Monmouth County, is the Union Hotel on Wharf Avenue. It was not built until 1791, but thereafter it served as a stagecoach inn. In the 1830s it saw a great deal of activity when James P. Allaire maintained a steamboat flotilla between his holdings in the county and New York. He put up at the Union Hotel and from there directed the traffic via Red Bank on the Shrewsbury River.

Speaking of Shrewsbury, the town of that name, also in Monmouth County, has the so-called Allen House on its main street. During the Revolution it was a tavern. The two-story structure with gambrel roof dates from 1667 and was the scene of bloody fighting during skirmishes in the village. Tories, hidden in the graveyard of nearby Christ Church, on one occasion attacked a group of unarmed Virginians leaving the tavern, killed three, and carried the rest off to prison in New York.

The American Hotel in Freehold was not established until 1824. It has survived almost a century and a half of change, from the days of stagecoaches and a country hostelry to the motor cars and dining ease of the present time. Always a gathering place for people from far and near who rallied for the trotting derbies and horse racing at Monmouth tracks, its walls are lined with a splendid collection of Currier & Ives prints. In addition, there are old dolls, carriages, and other toys of past generations along the corridors on the ground floor. The main taproom has memorabilia from the days when the horse was king and when old glassware and steins were always near at hand.

Mount Pleasant

On Route 79, also in Monmouth County, there stands, not far from Matawan, a remodeled building now called Poet's Inn. It is said to have been frequented during and after the Revolution by Philip Freneau and his friends when the firebrand pamphleteer was a scourge to the British and a great aid in stirring the patriotic fervor of dissenting colonists.

Orginally known as Mount Pleasant Tavern, it has a modern painting of Freneau hanging in the lobby. It is especially interesting because Freneau is known to have refused during his lifetime to sit for any artist. He is said to have turned down even Rembrandt Peale. Freneau lived for many years along the old road now known as Route 79 on the outskirts of a hamlet still known as Mount Pleasant. The house is on a hilltop and is in private hands. He died there in 1832 and is buried in a nearby graveyard, with a marble shaft to mark the spot.

South Jersey is literally filled with taverns dating from or before the Revolution, and after into the nineteenth century. There are many in Burlington, Mount Holly, Woodstown, Crosswicks, Camden, Gloucester City, Cape May City, and numerous places in between. It would require more space than I am prepared to give to list them, and then it is more than likely that I would fail to set down all of them.

The Revolution and fighting in South Jersey were striking events. I recall well a map of New Jersey on which the late John Alden, of SAR and Mayflower descent, listed nearly three hundred battles and skirmishes, many of them in South Jersey. It was his hobby, but he died before realizing his dream of publishing a work using his research.

Woodbury

Many innkeepers in the closing years of the eighteenth century were veterans of the Revolution. One was Robert

Taylor, who kept the Upper Tavern opposite the Quaker meeting house in Woodbury and had been a colonel in the Gloucester County Militia during the war.

Another prominent South Jerseyan was Josiah Hillman, who had been a lieutenant colonel in the Gloucester Militia. He took over the Middle Tavern in Woodbury, Gloucester County, in 1779, after it had been seized by the Commissioners of Forfeited Estates when the owner turned out to have Loyalist leanings. Almost immediately the Middle Tavern became a popular place under the direction of Colonel Hillman, and other forfeited property seized by the state was sold there. The Board of Freeholders for Gloucester County met there in early December 1786, and ordered the levying of 500 pounds sterling to pay for erecting the Gloucester County courthouse and jail.

Two years later, in 1788, Colonel Hillman left and was succeeded by Samuel Wood. Another two years followed and in 1790, according to license applications on file with the court, Wood was succeeded by two men, John Anderson and Joseph Hugg. The tavern was kept in 1808 by Mark Brown; later innkeepers indicated were Randall Sparks, Joseph B. Hillman, Samuel H. Runyan, and John Dunham.

It should be remembered that, during the Revolution, South Jersey was more heavily populated and industrialized than the northern part, largely because of the bog iron mining and the glass houses, both of which attracted large numbers of workers and their families. The British occupied Philadelphia and there was fighting on both sides of the Delaware, as well as up and down the river. Fighting within the state took place at Trenton, Princeton, and Monmouth, and also over the entire region.

Smithville

One of the better-known hostelries in Atlantic County during the nineteenth century was the Smithville Inn, located in the town of the same name. Restored in 1951, it operates as a dining place for people from a wide area and even from far-away Philadelphia. Much of the delightful atmosphere from Victorian days remains.

The story is told that, in the days when elections were somewhat more lively than now, Republicans and Democrats alike from the vicinity would gather at the Smithville Inn and stay throughout the hours awaiting final returns on Election Day. Sometimes there would be too much imbibing of strong drink, and tempers would flare. Local officials are reported to have put an end to the trouble by erecting a fence, or wooden barrier, dividing the field alongside the inn so the warring factions would be separated. Thus, according to tradition, came the saying "to mend political fences."

Cranbury

The Cranbury Inn in the Middlesex County town of that name was established in 1780. It stands today on the main street on the site of a much earlier tavern kept before 1753 by John Predmore, who advertised in that year that he "kept a good Stage-Waggon" to receive passengers and/or freight enroute from New York to Philadelphia. All during the stagecoach era the Cranbury Inn catered to passengers on the King's Highway, and when I visited the place the present proprietor, M. J. (Doc) D'Agostino, led me to a seat in the historic structure.

On the attractively prepared menu I noted carefully the following statement of welcome:

> You are dining today in a historically noted inn that will celebrate its bicentennial in less than a quarter-century. You are sitting where some of our country's famous founders enjoyed eating at the time of the inn's establishment—in 1780—and their fathers relaxed in the early 1700s, when John Predmore maintained an important post-

The Cranbury Inn in Cranbury, dated 1780. Photographed in 1973.
COURTESY RICHARD M. LEA.

house on the same site. Throughout the eighteenth century, Cranbury was a prosperous stopping-off place because the public highway, called King George's Road, was the key link between New England and the Southern colonies.

George Washington and many of his soldiers spent the night before the Battle of Monmouth in Cranbury, some of them at the old posthouse. Later, Congressional leaders, instrumental in launching the success of our democracy, stayed overnight at the "new" inn, then known as the United States Hotel, enroute to formative meetings in Boston, New York and Philadelphia. Now the name is changed, the faces are different and the public highway is elsewhere, but we hope you can still sense the colonial heritage that is here—and enjoy it as others did while making it."

On the way from Cranbury to Freehold, we pass through the quaint old community of Englishtown, on the main street of which is the Village Inn, operating as a shelter for weary travelers and a stagecoach stop since 1722. During the Revolution it was kept by a Daniel Herbert, who made chairs in his spare time and thus helped establish the famed early chairmaking industry in Monmouth County. It was headquarters for General Charles Lee and Lafayette before the Battle of Monmouth, and was visited by Washington. Later

New signpost outside Village Inn, Englishtown, tells history in few words. COURTESY RICHARD M. LEA.

Lee was court martialed at New Brunswick for ordering Continental troops to retreat at the Battle of Monmouth.

The Village Inn has changed very little over the years. It has been kept modernized, but little else. At one end of the long, low structure—its distinctive pillars supporting the long porch just a step above the street—there is set a varnished board contrasting vividly with the white clapboard. It shows the Village Inn and the establishing date of 1722. Inside, a separate door leads to living quarters for innkeeper and family, another to the inn itself, and still another to the taproom, where the long bar is seldom lacking local citizens, just as in olden times. Bedrooms upstairs are still kept ready for itinerants.

6

Tavern Customs and Menus

An idea of the scarcity of shelter for travelers in New Jersey during the colonial era, as well as the tavern customs of that period, is to be gained from the diary kept by the Rev. Carl Mangus Wrangel during a ten-day trip in October 1764 for some 220 miles across the state from Philadelphia to the Atlantic Ocean and back.

Granting that the South Jersey of that time was sparsely settled, his experiences are nevertheless quite typical of conditions existing throughout the East and West Jerseys of that day. Carl K. Anderson, an enthusiastic student of Swedish-American history, wrote an article for *New Jersey History,* a quarterly sponsored by the New Jersey Historical Society, which included excerpts from the diary. It recounts day by day how the Lutheran minister made his way on horseback over a thinly populated countryside to visit people who had not heard the Lord's word in many a year.

The Rev. Mr. Wrangel was accompanied only by Robert Friend Price, high sheriff of Gloucester County, who volunteered to show the way—particularly to the occasional Swedes who were in need of the word of God. The two men must have stayed for the most part with settlers along the path, because reference to taverns is meager and not too complimentary. The first mention, as a matter of fact, is on the second day out and is as follows:

> We continued our journey another ten miles to a tavern run by a man named Scull. This man, Scull, is a member of the English Church; he moved here from Egg Harber. Little or no knowledge of God appears to dwell in his house; however the people showed themselves to be attentive to my address on man's obligation so to care for the body that he does not completely forget the soul.

According to Mr. Anderson, the Scull Tavern, located in a hamlet now known as Berlin, was then called Long-a-Coming. It was on an old Indian trail leading to the seashore that later became known as Egg Harbor Road. The tavern was started, according to Anderson, about 1761 by Samuel Scull, and was kept by him, except for the three years from 1766 to 1769, until his death in 1777. The tavern is mentioned by the late Charles S. Boyer, an authority on the old inns and taverns of South Jersey, in his book on the subject.

The Rev. Mr. Wrangel also records in his diary that that same day the two men went "another nine miles to a tavern called the Blue Anchor, where we arrived at 1 o'clock. These people received me with great joy. The man is an Englishman named Mattocks, but his wife is a Swede named Keen and was from the Raccon congregation."

The Blue Anchor Tavern, according to Boyer, was located on the same Indian trail that led from the Delaware across the state to the shore. Raccon was changed long ago to Swedesboro. I have traveled the same road without finding trace of either tavern mentioned in the Wrangel diary. I am told by native residents, however, that they were the usual type of tavern for those days, consisting of two rooms on the ground floor, of which one held the bar and tables with chairs. A loft reached by ascending a ladder was overhead, used by chance travelers who stayed for the night.

At Little Egg Harbor the Rev. Mr. Wrangel and Sheriff Price, after prayers and breakfast at the home of an Irishman named Elisha Clark with whom they had spent the night, went for a stroll. Telling of what they saw, the Rev. Mr. Wrangel says:

> There was a tavern run by an Irishman by the name of Wescott, who appeared to be making money to the harm of others and with little concern about God. At 10 o'clock the people gathered, and when we got to the church, we found it completely filled with the seafolk and laborers who live here.

Wescott's tavern was located at a settlement known as the Forks, near Batsto. I find that it was kept by Colonel Richard Wescott from 1761 until 1781, when he moved to May's Landing.

Much of what is known about taverns in New Jersey, and about customs as well as food, is derived from old diaries of Englishmen and Frenchmen who visited the state and toured her taverns prior to, or soon after, the early 1800s. They seemed to delight in setting down the many such places they stayed and the unusual events they encountered.

Henry Wansey of England was one of the numerous foreigners to visit here. In 1794 he commented on the mosquitoes that infested the meadows in the vicinity of Newark, declaring that "they burst from their fullness." Speaking of Newark, he expressed a liking "for this pleasant little country town" and added: "After a warming dish of tea at the Hounds and Horn (Gifford's) I walked throughout the town. The First Church was particularly elegant and I climbed to the roof top gallery for a view as far as New York."

Thomas Twining was another Englishman who liked what he saw. He visited Jersey's inns in 1795, according to old diaries now in the New Jersey Historical Society Library. According to one of his many entries in that year, "the rooms were good and the service splendid." Speaking of Newark, he referred to "fine white houses on the Western hillside" and asserted that "if I settled in America I should be induced to prefer that spot to any other I have seen."

The Duke de la Rochefaucault, a Frenchman, was also a visitor in 1795. Then there was John Davis from England in 1798, and the memorable visit of the Marquis de Lafayette early in the 1800s.

According to Richard B. Morris in *American Heritage* for December 1971, Benjamin Franklin and John Adams, most unlikely bedfellows, shared a small room in an unidentified New Brunswick inn the late summer of 1776. They were on the way from Philadelphia by order of the Continental Congress, accompanied by Edward Rutledge of South Carolina, to meet for an informal peace conference on Staten Island with the brothers Lord Richard and Sir William Howe.

Franklin did not get so far in his unfinished autobiography as to recall the occasion, but, Morris writes, Adams recorded the night's adventure in his diary, in which he says that the room, scarcely large enough for a bed and grudgingly provided by the innkeeper, had a single window. The window was open and Adams recalls that he was afraid of the mild September night air and got out of bed to close it.

"Don't shut the window. We shall be suffocated, "Franklin remonstrated, according to Adams, who explained his fear of night air. His senior companion reassured him: "The air within the chamber will soon be, and indeed is now, worse than without doors. Come, open the window and come to bed, and I will convince you. I believe you are not acquainted with my theory of colds." With some misgivings, he records, Adams agreed to open the window. While Franklin continued to expound his theory of the causes of colds, Adams says he fell asleep, remembering that the last words he heard were spoken very drowsily.

Ordinaries were out of the picture in New Jersey well before the end of the seventeenth century. Even governing groups such as the courts began to use the word *tavern* instead of *ordinary*. Seldom were they referred to as inns and it was only after the American Revolution that *house* became popular, along with the prefix of *Washington* or some other worthy name. It was barely 150 years ago that hotels came into being, when the first such establishment in the state was opened at Cape May.

There was no putting on of airs or exclusiveness at Jersey taverns of the 1700s. Manners were rude even into the next century. All travelers sat at the same table. Frequently the rooms were double-bedded, and four or more who were complete strangers often slept together. After a weary traveler was fast asleep, the landlord was quite likely to enter the room, candle in hand, escorting a stranger who calmly shared the bed until morning. Travel had increased with the years, and the public houses had not been built with that in mind. At any rate, the sexes were kept rigidly separate on the few occasions when women were obliged to travel. Anyone who objected to a strange bedfellow of the same sex was considered obnoxious and unreasonably fastidious.

In a book now out of print called *Notions of Americans,* the French author, writing of experiences during the triumphal tour of the Marquis de Lafayette of the United States in 1824, had this to say about Bispham's Tavern in Trenton:

> We were received by the landlord with perfect civility, but without the slightest shade of obsequiousness. The deportment of the innkeeper was manly, courteous and even kind; but there was that in his air which sufficiently proved that both parties were expected to manifest the same qualities. We were asked if we all formed one

party, or whether the gentlemen who alighted from stage number one wished to be by themselves. We were shown into a neat well-furnished little parlour, where our supper made its appearance in about twenty minutes. The table contained many little delicacies, such as game, oysters, and choice fish, and several things were named to us as at hand if needed.

The tea was excellent, the coffee, as usual, indifferent enough. The papers of New York and Philadelphia were brought at our request, and we sat with our two candles before a cheerful fire reading them as long as we pleased. Our bed chambers were spacious, well furnished and as neat as possible; the beds as good as one finds them out of France. Now for these accommodations, which were just as good with one solitary exception [sanitary] as you would meet in the better order of British provincial inns, and much better in the quality and abundance of the food, we paid the sum of 4s 6d each.

Certain it is that some Jersey taverns had come a long way in less than a century. This same author says he stopped at some fifty such places during the tour, some not quite so good as, but others better than Bispham's.

Under the date August 8, 1682, the Burlington County court's earliest available records indicate that it took cognizance of the prices, high for that day, charged by keepers of spiritous drink. A resolution adopted at that time said that it was:

Ordered by ye Cort that no Person or Persons keeping or shall keep an Ordinary or Inne within ye Jurisdiction of this Cort shall from after ye Tenth day of August inst. take more than Two pence for an Ale Quart of good wholesome Ale, or strong Beere, and Benj. West and Henry Grubb are by ye Cort appointed to be Ale Tasters and to see to ye measures for Ale & Beere, according to ye order above, until ye next General Assembly, or further orders.

Neither Benjamin West nor Henry Grubb is further identified. Needless to say, they must have been men of prominence in the community.

On February 20, 1683, the same court ordered that "cider" should not be offered at more than four pence per quart and rum at more than 1s 6d for the same quantity. That was followed on August 19, 1739, by an order fixing the prices of a long list of "victuals" for the guidance of innkeepers and customers alike.

Black bread and a bowl of porridge was the standard breakfast served at some Jersey taverns through most of the 1700s. Others went for more elaborate fare from nearby vegetable garden, barnyard, or river. By the 1870s and 1880s, the taverns and other public houses catering to the vacationer, or summer boarder in particular, literally outdid themselves in the way of meals. At Princess Bay, near Long Branch, there was a dining place that frequently entertained such celebrities of the time as Lillian Russell, "Diamond Jim" Brady, Jim Fiske, and others from nearby hostelries. Besides clamming, fishing, and "bowling on the green" for entertainment, meals were lavish enough to excite the palate of a visiting potentate. A typical bill of fare for breakfast listed steamed or roasted clams, Spanish mackerel, sea bass, weakfish, blue fish, stewed terrapin, Maryland fried chicken, corn fritters, waffles, and potatoes done in any of several ways. Luncheon and dinner menus were equally alluring.

Meeting at Trenton on March 5, 1722, the Court of Quarter Sessions of Hunterdon County adopted the following resolution, according to the records of the court for that date:

> Ordered by the Cort that All publique houses in this County shall pay obedience and duly observe and keep All the Directions of prices of liquors And other things contained in sd. order which shall here After be exprest by the particulars, And that the clerks of the County shall record the same and give a copy to each publique house proprietor in the County. And they shall hang up the same in some publique place in their severall houses so that all Travelers and others may have Recourse thereto. And that it shall remain on the penalty of the forfiture of their licenses in case of default—viz., as follows, the prices all to be proclamation money.

After that long harangue, on a second sheet was listed the following:

	d	s		d	s
"To every Hott Dinor——————7d		½			
Ditto cold as Breakfast and Supper———————				4d	½
Maderia Wine per pint—————————————					11
Hot dito per pint————————————————				1d	
D. Caneroy Mamsey or white wine per pint————				1	3
D. Hott Mamsey or white wine per pint———————				1	6
D. tealls wine per pint——————————————					7
D. Claret wine per pint——————————————				1	3
Metheglin per pint————————————————					6
Rum per gill————————————————————				3d	
D. Hott per gill————————————————————				4d	
Rume punch per quart fower gills of rum in it					
Made with Muskevado Shewgar—1d					8
Made of duble refined Shewager—ditto					
Brandy per gill———————————————					2½
Brandy punch per quart fower gills of brandy					
Made of Muskevado Shewgar——————————				3d	
Made of Duble refined Shewgar—3d					2
And so for a greater or Lesser quantity in proportion of Brandy or Rum punch					
Poor per quart—————————————————					4
Bristol or London beer per bottle—1d					3
Syder per quart——————————————————					3
Lodging per night—————————————————					3
Horse pasturage per night——————————————					4½
Standingall Hay per night——————————————					4½
Oats per peck————————————————————					9
Indian corn per peck—————————————————				1d	
Bran per peck————————————————————					3

Responding to complaints concerning people who sold liquor without license, the Hunterdon County Court adopted the following resolution in May 1734:

> Upon the petition of divers of Inhabitants of the Town of Lebanon setting forth that William Phillips of the sd. town retails liquors by small measure and keeps a disorderly House & it appearing to this Court that the sd. Wm. Phillips has no Lycence granted him to keep a Publick House of Entertainment, it's ordered by the Court that Justice Martin Ryderson & Justice John Van Sickle do inquire into the Truth of the allegation of the said Petition; & if the said justices shall think it convenient they may suppress the said Publick House & order the sd. William Phillips to retail no more strong liquors by small measures.

Such was the manner in which Hunterdon County courts endeavored, in the eighteenth century, to police the non-licensee. In 1792 they authorized the city council of Trenton alone to issue licenses and renewals, keeping for themselves jurisdiction over all other taverns in Hunterdon County.

In 1812 the committee of Deptford Township met at the tavern of James Smith in Woodbury "to count the vote for township officers." According to a bill for expenses rendered by Smith and paid for by the township, the members of the committee fared pretty well. The bill follows:

Deptford Township Dr. to Jesse Smith
March 12, 1812

TO	½ gill Gin————————————————	$.06
	1 pint Lisbon Wine————————————	.50
	¾ pint of Gin————————————————	.25
	¾ pint of Gin————————————————	.25
	½ pint of Gin————————————————	.06¼
	6 Diners————————————————————	3.00
	½ pint of Brandy at Diner—————————	.25
	2 Mugs Beere————————————————	.25

½ pints of spirits at Diner—————————	.25
½ pint gin at Diner——————————————	.25
Segars————————————————————	.18
½ pint Gin—————————————————	.25
½ pint Gin—————————————————	.25
8 suppers @ 37½ cents—————————	3.00
	$8.81

At the Cannonball House, maintained by the Scotch Plains-Fanwood Historical Society, there is a well-thumbed copy of *The Cook's Oracle and Housekeeper's Manual,* published by J. & J. Harper, 82 Cliff St., N.J.C. in 1830. It was used in that year and later by operators of the Historic Inn, just across the street, in Scotch Plains. The inn was a stopping place on the Swift Sure Stage Line running at that time along the Old York Road from Elizabethtown Point to Philadelphia.

In the library of the New Jersey Society, SAR, now quartered in the pre-Revolutionary Bonnell House in Elizabeth, there is the following declaration of a Revolutionary War veteran with regard to his experience at a north Jersey tavern in the early 1800s:

> I pray'd her to show me where I must lodge. She conducted mee to a parlour in a little back Leanto, which was almost filled with the bedstead, which was so high that I was forced to climb on a chair to gitt up to ye wretched bed that lay on it, on which having Strecht my tired Limbs and Lay'd my Head on a Sad-coloured pillow, I began to think of the transactions of ye past day.

7

Stagecoaches and Post Roads

The first stagecoaches on Jersey highways, or on what passed for roads in those days, were merely heavy covered wagons, with planks arranged crossways to serve as most uncomfortable seats for passengers. They were without springs and the seats had no backs.

It was a two-day trip from Elizabethtown Point on Staten Island Sound to Philadelphia by any of several possible routes. Small wonder that the few passengers needed help when descending to the ground after a wearing, bone-jarring experience along the "open road"!

Most of the travel was at first on horseback and continued to be for years. During the years of fighting during the Revolution, the travel in New Jersey by officers and those on official business was done on horseback. That was of course the mode of travel from New Brunswick to Rocky Hill of the courier who in late 1783 debarked from ship at the former port and hurried to tell Washington at the Berrien Mansion the news of the signing of the treaty at Ghent, which officially ended the American Revolution. He then went on to notify the Continental Congress meeting in Nassau Hall at Princeton.

Chairs were long the favorite way for men, and sometimes women, to get about during pioneer days and even into the 1800s. These people had social standing and position, and they rebelled at the crudely made coaches where they were jostled about with total strangers. Frequently they had slaves, or employes, who grasped bars front and rear as a means of hoisting the precious load to shoulder height. In such fashion the gently swaying chair was above the rough trail or roadway.

As a matter of fact, Benjamin Scudder, farmer and gristmill operator along the banks of the Rahway River near Springfield, noted on the margin of his almanac diary as late as 1820 that he made several necessary trips to New York City "by chair."[1]

When roads were widened in the mid-1700s for the first stagecoaches and high cantilevered wagons, they were so rutfilled in the rainy seasons and dusty in the summer sun that long trips were avoided whenever possible. Horseback and chair were two ways often preferred to avoid such troubles.

It is well here to describe the terms *horseback* and *chair.* The rider on horseback merely had to know how to mount and ride. The saddle was all-important, and papers or documents were stowed away in saddlebags of either leather or canvas slung across the back of the animal directly behind the rider.

Very few chairs have survived the passing years. I have seen less than half a dozen. Excellent examples are in the New Jersey Historical Society building in Newark and the State Museum in Trenton. Frequently they were closed on three sides and open at the front. Some of them had low half-doors, movable so as to swing back and allow a passenger to

1. The original Scudder diaries are in the Rutgers University Library at New Brunswick and photocopies are in the New Jersey Historical Society Library in Newark.

alight. A very few, according to the record, had a full door for the utmost privacy. The more crudely made ones had only leather covers at the rear-and sides, with a plain board seat inside. The more ornate were heavily padded or quilted on both sides of the seat. Frequently contrasting colors, even in leather, were used.

It was the custom for many years to have employees at each inn or tavern always at hand to help travelers alight from coaches and wagons after having undergone the rigors of the open road. When guests of special importance were expected or departing, the landlord personally performed the honors. He either stayed by the arriving guest until he was able to walk alone, or bade farewell to the departing traveler with lavish pleas for his early return.

As before stated, the first stagecoaches were nothing more than covered wagons, with planks placed crossways as seats without backs. By the time the Old York Road was opened across Jersey from Paulus Hook to Philadelphia, via ferry at Coryll's Crossing (Lambertville), stages had already appeared on the Old Mine Road across a part of Sussex County, on the King's Highway out of Elizabethtown Point, and on some roads in South Jersey. The famed Concord stagecoach was the first through neighboring Pennsylvania. It had padded seats, with backs and leather strip suspensions from the body of the vehicle to the bar connecting the front and rear wheels. They were a great improvement over the cruder wagons used as stages in the late 1600s and on into the mid-1700s.

The wheels of the improved Concords were oftentimes as much as six feet in height and the coach body was slung low between them. Nevertheless, the passengers needed a high box to either dismount or climb aboard a stage. It was many years before coaches, and later even carriages, were sufficiently low to permit getting on or off directly from or to the ground. I do not doubt for a moment that the oldtime stepping stone in use through the Victorian era and sometimes seen on quiet streets today originated in those times.

The oldtime stagecoaches were pulled by two, four, and even six horses in tandem, with the driver seated on his perch atop the vehcile. The opening chapter of *The Story of an Old Farm* by the late Andrew Mellick, Jr., tells of his ride from Somerville to Pluckemin and beyond in the following words:

> Squeezing in on the front seat by the driver's side, our feet were inextricably entangled in mail bags, bundles, whiffletrees and horses' tails. The stage is loaded up with three or four [passengers] to each seat and, with a mountain of luggage piled high behind, we started noisily down the main street.

Snell's *History of Hunterdon and Somerset Counties,* earlier referred to, tells many interesting stories of travel in stagecoach days on the Old York Road, which was not open its entire length until 1764. One such yarn tells of the arrival of a stagecoach as follows:

> Thus came the great chariot tearing down the street of the town or village, behind the magnificent, foaming horses, spurred on by the blast of a bugle. The crash of the wheels of the towering equipage, the splendid connecting link between the two great cities of New York and Philadelphia, was inspiring and electrifying to everybody.

The Swift Sure Stage Line, one of many operating on the Old York Road during its heyday, was organized in 1769, five years after the highway was open. The Swift Sure Line soon became the leading through-operator on the road and for years maintained a thirty-hour schedule. The single overnight stop was at first at Centerville. Later, travelers were bedded down in Flemington, where they were put up at the old Union Hotel. There were frequent stops for change of horses, rest, and even lunch.

In 1769, the same year of founding, the Swift Sure Stage Line ran the following advertisement in the *New York Gazette and Post Boy:*

> A new stage line is to be erected to go from New York to Philadelphia via Powles Hook, from thence through Newark and Elizabethtown to Bound Brook and the North Branch of the Raritan to Coryll's Ferry, the only ferry between Newark and Philadelphia noted for its shortness and convenience over the river Delaware.
>
> Stages will leave the Barley Sheaf Tavern at eight in the morning and arrive at Wells' Ferry (later Coryll's) twelve hours later. There will be stops for refreshments and to change horses every ten miles.

In 1827, when round trips were made three times each week, the fare one way was twenty shillings, at that time about five dollars. The Swift Sure Stage Line the year before had won a government contract to carry the mail. Numerous short-haul stage lines started over the years, the last being the Raritan & Somerville Line, which operated until 1898, according to the *Somerset Messenger,* published at the time in Somerville.

As a small boy at the turn of the century, I rode in an old-fashioned stagecoach to Sunday school at the Scotch Plains Baptist Church. It circled North and Martine Avenues and carried worshipers from Fanwood Borough along Martine Avenue past the Stage Coach Inn at the corner of Front Street and Park Avenue (an extension of Martine) to church at Park Avenue and Grand Street. It ran only on Sunday, and for how long I do not know. Undoubtedly the idea of a stage line came from the Swift Sure Stage Line and the proximity of the old inn.

Occasionally I was privileged to sit on the box alongside Louis Coddington, the driver. He drove a team of two matched sorrels. I was enthralled to watch him guide the horses by means of a squirt from a cud of tobacco held in his mouth, well directed at the ear of the lead animal.

ADVERTISEMENTS.

The Swiftsure Line of Stages,

Running from New York and Philadelphia,

By the shortest, cheapest, safest, and most pleasant road,

Through Newark, Springfield, Scotch-Plains, Union Camp, Bound-book, Millstone, Pennington, Newtown, Bustleton, and Frankford.

THE SWIFTSURE

Starts from New-York at 9 o'clock every day (Sundays excepted) and arrives at Philadelphia, early the next evening.

From Philadelphia it starts from the Green Tree, No. 50 North Fourth street, at 8 o'clock every morning, and arrives at New York early the next evening.

Fare for passengers 5 dollars, way passengers 6 cents per mile. Each passenger allowed 14lb of baggage. One hundred and fifty weight of baggage to pay the same as a passenger.

All baggage to be at the risk of the owner, unless insured and receipted for by the clerks of the different offices. Rate of insurance one per cent.

*** Apply to WILLIAM VANDERVOORT, No. 48 Courtland Street, N. E. Corner of Greenwich Street, New York, and to JOHN M'CALLA, No. 50 North Fourth Street Philadelphia.

JUST

Advertisement of the Swift Sure Stage Line in The Rush Light, *March 31, 1800. COURTESY THE NEW YORK HISTORICAL SOCIETY.*

Back in 1794, when John Mercereau and his stagecoach—called quite appropriately the Flying Machine—made bi-weekly trips along the King's Highway, from Paulus Hook to Philadelphia, he was proud to keep on schedule, according to Daniel Van Winkle's *Story of Old Bergen*. Written nearly 150 years later, it tells how old John would rein in his four-horse hitch near the entrance to the Merchants' and Drovers' Tavern on the outskirts of present-day Rahway and announce:

> Ten minutes allowed. We travel according to schedule. Must be in New Brunswick by noon, on the dot. Enjoy comforts of the tavern while you may. Be at your ease. The Flying Machine is always on the dot.

Stagecoaches ran daily between New York and Newark and Philadelphia. The return trip to Philadelphia left Cortland Street and Broadway, in New York City, at 3 P.M. each afternoon. It left Broad and Market Streets, in Newark, at 6 A.M., according to a copy of a schedule in the New York Historical Society. The document reads:

Ye Old Stage Coach—"The Flying Machine"
  Schedule—New York to Philadelphia
Stage—Leaves New York, corner of Cortland
  Street and Broadway, at 5 A.M.
Ferry across North River to Pulis Hook. Time
  required: one hour and thirty minutes.
Breakfast at Gifford House, Newark, at 7 A.M.
Dinner at Brunswick, 12 noon.
Supper and to bed, Princeton.
Leaves Princeton at 5 A.M.; arrives
  Philadelphia at 12 noon.
Time on road: nineteen hours of actual travel.
Price per passenger: from Paulis Hook to Princeton,
  10 shillings. Ferriage free. Three pence per mile
  for any intermediate travel

A broadside in the files of the New York Historical Society signed Mercereau & John Barnhill and addressed to "The Public" reads as follows:

> That the Stage Wagons kept by John Barnhill in Elm Street, in Philadelphia, and John Mercereau at the New Blazing Star, near New York, continue their Stages in Two Days from Powles Hook Ferry, opposite New York, to Philadelphia; return from Philadelphia to Powles Hook in Two Days also; they well endeavor to oblige the Public by keeping the best of Wagons and sober Drivers, and set out from New York and Philadelphia on Mondays and Thursdays, punctually at Sunrise, and meet at Prince Town the same nights to exchange Passengers, and each returne the day after. Those that are kind enough to Encourage the Undertaking are desired to cross the Powles-Hook Ferry the Evening before, as they must set off early. The Price for each Passenger is Ten Shillings to Prince-Town, and from thence to Philadelphia Ten Shillings more, Ferriage free. There will be but two Wagons, but four sets of fresh horses so that it will be very safe for any Person to send Goods, as there are but two Drivers, they may exchange their Goods without any Mistake. Persons may now go from New York to Philadelphia and back again in five Days and remain in Philadelphia two Nights and one Day to do their business in:The Public may be assured that any other to Philadelphia and regular Stages will be kept by the Publick's obliged humble Servants.

Matthias Ward started one of the first stage lines out of Newark in the early 1760s. He took advantage of the road that entered the town over what is now Ferry Street. It connected, in Newark, with an extension of the Brunswick-to-Trenton and the Old York roads. It enabled travelers to pass over an all-land-and-ferry route all the way from the Hudson River, opposite Manhattan Island, to the Delaware River and Philadelphia. At the same time it allowed for either stops or starts at Newark; the value to that town's future was a major development.

Ward's stage line also ran to Paulus Hook and thus gave Newark a direct connection with New York. Prosperity caused Ward to take John Thompson as a partner in 1768 and, according to the files of the New Jersey Historical

Society, he advertised "a new plan for stage wagons." It called for dispatching two stages every day except Sunday, one starting westward from Paulus Hook, with its terminal at the Rising Sun Tavern in Newark. The other stage went east from the tavern to Paulus Hook.

The partners cautioned all travelers to be "prompt as the wagons must be very exact in meeting Captain Berry's ferry at the Hackensack River." Travelers were assured that "they may depend on constant attendance and good usuage." Traffic was so heavy that the partners prospered and there were four rival stage lines soon competing for the business. They all promised a two-day service from New York to Philadelphia via Newark. Abraham Skillman's broadside advertised the trip in only a day and one-half, a schedule that the record shows he maintained most of the time.

The first road in the state, and quite likely the entire country as it is now constituted, was laid out by Dutch settlers. That was in the mid-1600s. It started at Esopus (Kingston, N.Y.) on the Hudson River and crossed into New Jersey near Port Jervis, on the way to the Delaware River. The original purpose was to provide a route to the copper mines opened at Pahaquarry, near the Delaware, by the Dutch so that ore from the mines could be gotten overland to ocean-going ships tied up in the Hudson.[2]

Settlements along the Old Mine Road soon provided numerous inns and other public houses for the occasional traveler, but when the 1600s came to an end and the mines shut down, the region returned pretty much to the wilderness it had been formerly, particularly in the Jersey portion. Now

2. The Tock Island project sponsored by the Federal Government, to dam the Delaware River and create an immense recreation area, will flood parts of the Old Mine Road and large sections of neighboring countryside. The best work I have read on the subject of the Old Mine Road is entitled THE OLD MINE ROAD, by the late C. G. Hines after he had traversed the entire highway on foot in the early 1900s.

modern concrete roads cross over the Pahaquarry area and thousands of motorists go each year to view the wonders of the Delaware Water Gap, giving no thought to the history thereof.

The 1700s saw new and extensive use of the Lower Road from Burlington to the ferry at Amboy. Then there was "the Old Dutch Road" that ran from Elizabethtown Point through Woodbridge, Piscataway, and Inian's Ferry (New Brunswick), down the Delaware River to what is now Trenton. A road, or trail, also followed the north branch of the Raritan River. Starting at Staten Island Sound, it was called, appropriately enough, the Raritan Road, and still exists today along the same meandering course.

Those first few roads for the most part followed old Indian trails. In 1676 the General Assembly of East Jersey ordered a road built from Piscataway to Middletown. Again, in 1683, it provided for "the planning of highways, bridges, passages, landings and ferries," but authority was lacking to levy taxes to pay for such work, and it was years before anything was accomplished.

In 1681 and again in 1684, the General Assembly of West Jersey passed several measures for the laying out of roads connecting the settlements along the Delaware River. In consequence, new highways began to branch out across the southern part of the state by the time the century had ended. Word was slow, however, with labor provided in large part by local farmers. Time for such work was limited by act of the General Assembly to six days a year, and it was usually performed at times when chores were slack around the farm. It was difficult to more than scratch the surface.

One of the best reports on the condition of early New Jersey roads that I have read was written by George Fox, famed Quaker and traveler of the late 1600s. In an entry in his diary dated June 27, 1672, he tells of his party's leaving

Middletown for Shrewsbury, both in Monmouth County. He wrote:

> We rode for miles through the woods and many bad bogs, one worse than the other. The descent was so steep that we were fain to slide down with our horses and then let them lie and breathe themselves before they go on. This place the people call Purgatory.

Fox was one of the first itinerant preachers to travel over so-called roads in what is now New Jersey. His diary reflects the conditions existing then and for many years thereafter. Monmouth County has changed greatly in the three centuries since then. There is no place now known as Purgatory. Some natives believe Fox's reference was figurative, made to the swamps even now existing on the Swimming River, along the road of that name in the vicinity of Lincroft.

Efforts to widen those early roads caused big holes where tree stumps had been pulled out, and great rocks were further hazards. In the rainy season, holes and ruts filled with water. Summer heat brought dust to cake on travelers, with the added plague of mosquitoes and flies in low places and at every river or stream crossing. In winter the so-called roads of North Jersey were barely passable; in South Jersey conditions were hardly better.

By the time the Old York Road was opened across the state, there had been some improvement in the most-traveled highways, but it was many years before the country lanes were any better. But neither time nor distance meant anything in those times. Often roads took a zigzag course up and down sharp rises or declines, or entirely skirted other difficult terrain. Man and beast were of first concern.

Writing for a Revolutionary History of Elizabeth prepared in 1926 by the city's sesquicentennial committee, the late B. J. Steib noted the following under the caption "Roads Thru Elizabeth":

During the Revolutionary War period, years 1775 to 1783, we had several roads running through our city, namely:

Road to Williams' farm, which in part is now called Colonial Road; Magie Road, which still holds its name; Road to Trotter's Mill, which is now called Elmora Avenue to Chilton Street, and North Avenue from Chilton Street to the city line.

Road from the Barracks to Springfield is now Cherry Street. Road from Stone Bridge [over Elizabeth River] to Newark is now called Broad Street to railroad junction [overpass had not been built] and then North Broad Street to city line. A road running from North Broad Street to Jewell's Mills is now called Salem Avenue. A road running from the Stone Bridge and called the Road to Woodruff's Farms is now called Mary Street.

The street now known as West Jersey Street was in part the Road to Williams' Farm and ran to Galloping Hill Road. East Jersey Street ran from Broad Street to Spring Street and had an outlet through Spring Street to Elizabeth Avenue. It did not continue beyond Spring Street.

There was one other road running to Woodruff's Farms which is now called Madison Avenue, to Magnolia Avenue and Meadows Street from there on. Woodruff's Farms were located on Meadows Street and Neck Lane. The road running from Broad Street to Staten Island Sound was called Road from the Court House to Elizabethtown Point. This road is now covered by Elizabeth Avenue to High Street; First Avenue from High to Third streets, and again Elizabeth Avenue from Third Street to the waterfront [Staten Island Sound].

The road to Halstead's Point, which was formerly called Luke Watson's Point, is now the point where Thompson's Creek, or Morse's Creek, now empties into Staten Island Sound. The Upper Road, or Country Road, to Rahway which ran from the Barracks Road, now Cherry Street, is now called Rahway Avenue. The Lower to Rahway ran from Pearl Street to Routinghouse Lane. This lane ran between the upper and lower roads to Rahway.

It is unfortunate that Steib did not identify Rahway as Bridge Town, the name by which it was first called. Also, the main road from Elizabethtown to Rahway was long known as the King's Highway, and before that as St. Georges' Avenue.

For some unknown reason, Steib also neglected to mention either Morris Avenue or Westfield Avenue, two leading thoroughfares even to this day. Morris Avenue was known in Revolutionary War days as the Road to Springfield.

It was the route taken by the British in seeking a way to get at Washington's forces through "the Short Hills," which brought on the battles of Springfield and Connecticut Farms. It is also famous as the first toll road in the country, by reason of an act in the Legislature in 1801.[3]

Westfield Avenue led to "the West Fields of Elizabethtown" and settlers of early Elizabethtown went there in summer to escape the intense heat and humidity along the Staten Island Sound shore front.

The roads in New Jersey during the Revolutionary War are well marked in the map collections of the New York Historical Society, which include most of those drawn by General Robert Erskine, who was Washington's first cartographer and surveyor general. Erskine, a Scotsman by birth, was sent to America to head the mines at Ringwood. His life is the subject of *The Lost General*, written in 1928 by Albert H. Heusser, then a Paterson newspaperman.

General Erskine found the roads in New Jersey little suited for Washington to oppose the British. His deputy and the second surveyor general under Washington was Simeon DeWitt, who took over when Erskine died in October 1780. DeWitt also knew a great deal about Jersey roads, both existing and lacking. Many of the maps in the Erskine collection were drawn and are signed by DeWitt.

When the 1800s arrived, Jersey roads, under the impetus of passenger and freight travel across and within the state, became more numerous and were even improved. During his long tenure, Governor Bloomfield was mainly concerned with fostering turnpikes. According to files of the New Jersey Historical Society, he caused the Legislature to grant more than fifty franchises between 1801 and 1829. It became almost a

---

3. I noted this fact in an article in the Newark Sunday News back in 1965, under the heading "Appeal of Antiques."

racket. Morris Avenue became the Number One toll road in the nation. Starting in Elizabethtown, it ran through Morristown and Newton before reaching Milford, on the Delaware River. Those early turnpikes, as they were called, paved the way for the contemporary highway system.

Cornelius Vermeule, a surveyor who laid out and was first owner of the Blue Hills Plantation just west of present Plainfield in Union County, had a great deal to do with the early roads in New Jersey. He was called on frequently by Washington and Erskine when problems arose, and he is credited with plotting for the Old York Road as well as other early major highways. The Blue Hills Plantation is no more. Only the ancient burial ground, surrounded by a brick wall and with headstones dating from the 1760s, remains. Occasionally the old cemetery is cleared by Boy Scouts.

8

Wayside Signs and Symbols

Painted and sometimes carved signboards and figures always marked the early taverns or public houses. They were colorful adjuncts to daily life in New Jersey and also lent an important sense of direction to the weary traveler looking for a place to stop and get refreshments, or put up for the night.

They were indispensable to the Jerseyan of the eighteenth and nineteenth centuries. Before streets were named and had numbered dwellings and shops, and at a time when few could read anyway, people in all walks of life depended on signs. They attracted customers and inquirers alike. Nowadays patience and a calculating eye are necessary to spot one of the old signboards, and even then a long search is to be expected.

As education improved, advertisements in newspapers or simple familiarity with the neighborhood came to replace many of the old signs. But it was an early condition for granting a license to a keeper of a public house for the courts of both East and West Jersey to require that the licensee must erect a signboard in close proximity to his place. As a matter of fact, licenses granted even before the Revolution (I have inspected them by the hundred) included that stipulation.

Marker on Lambertville Inn, Lambertville, in 1973.

When the turn of the present century brought electricity and, later, neon lights, the old signs came to be considered a nuisance and even a danger, to the extent that most local ordinances curbed their use. Insurance is frequently required of owners because of peril to passersby. Tavern, inn, and hotel signs remain only in rural or less-populated areas and these, too, may soon disappear. But signboards or figures for early public houses were familiar to the colonists and even went westward with the first settlers. A tavern opened in Jerseyville, Illinois, back in 1840 had such a sign.

It is almost impossible to identify the craftsmen who were responsible for those early signs. In the first place, they soon became weatherbeaten and needed repainting, at which time traces of name or initials and date vanished. Then, too, the itinerant artist who probably did the original job was no longer available and the landlord either performed the task as best he could or called a local man.

The diary of Joel Barlow, as recounted in a book entitled *Yankee Odyssey* by James Woodress, tells of his stay at a North Jersey tavern without identifying the precise location. Barlow, an officer and preacher with Washington in winter camp at Jocky Hollow, was recuperating from a serious illness. One day the landlord asked him to try his hand at painting a signboard for the tavern. He did such a fine job in painting a scene of distant hills and lettering the tavern name that the landlord declined to accept payment for either room or board.

It is doubtful whether any of the signboards from colonial or even later days have survived. There are a few allegedly from those times in the New Jersey Historical Society in Newark, the Rutgers University Library in New Brunswick, and in private museums, but I very much doubt that they are original. The Mercer Museum in Doylestown, Pennsylvania, dating from 1916, has a Jersey sign, of the Crossed Keys Hotel of Trenton. Quite fittingly, it shows two crossed keys above the word *Hotel;* also, quite obviously it has been painted over several times.

The tavern sign often was only a board painted with the hostelry's name, but many times it was quite elaborate. It was attached to a wooden or wrought-iron frame, or arm, fashioned much like a fireplace crane. It usually projected from a corner of the tavern or from a post set in the front yard. The more crudely made ones were often fastened to a nearby tree or the fence surrounding the property, depending on the landlord's whim.

Stockton Inn signpost, Stockton, in 1973.

Occasionaly the sign was suspended from a substantial frame set in front of the tavern and in such cases a weather vane was likely to surmount one of the posts. It seems to have been a habit among Jersey's tavern keepers to move around, and often they took the signboard with them to the new location. Thus we find the King's Arms Tavern, apparently a very popular name in colonial Jersey, first in Trenton and then in Perth Amboy. In colonial times nearly every town or settlement had its King's Arms Tavern. After the

Revolution, the fad was to have the Washington House; later the Washington Hotel became popular.

Signboards took all manner of form and name to reflect the tavern or its owner's desires. The names are legion and the signs equally as numerous. The King's Arms Tavern called for a signboard showing the reigning head of Great Britain. Then there was the Bull's Head Tavern and a sign with a painting of a bull's head. The Wheat Sheaf Inn on St. George's Avenue Rosselle, had a sign with a sheaf of wheat painted on it. Only when a tavern or inn bore the owner's name was there a chance to use imagination, which as often as not resulted in the likeness of a horse's head, or the entire figure of the animal, or perhaps a rustic country scene.

The Red Lion Inn in Elizabethtown had a signboard with a lion on it in bright red. The Three Crowns Tavern in the same town had three crowns of equal size painted in bright gold or yellow. The King George Inn at Mt. Bethel is one of the few taverns I know of with the name on a signboard over the doorway, and it has been kept in that position since 1685.

The Revolution led to a postwar change in the naming of taverns. Anything referring to the crowned heads of Europe was, of course, taboo. The name was changed so as to do honor to Washington, Lafayette, or another equally famous patriot.

The early tavern keeper did not go in much for advertising. I have searched the files of newspapers in New Jersey and, before they were printed in this state, in Philadelphia and New York, without finding direct reference to them. It is odd, though, that craftsmen in the various trades frequently referred to their location as near or next to such-and-such a tavern. I have in mind the clockmakers, silversmiths, and others, who gave their former locations in Philadelphia and New York as near the Blazing Star or Roaring Bull Tavern; in Jersey they were next door to or across from the Sign of the

New Jersey College in Princeton, the Red Lion Inn in Elizabethtown, or any of the many taverns elsewhere in the state.

After the 1750s, when stagecoach lines were seeking business, cards began to appear in the press announcing a stop for change of horses, or refreshment, at any of numerous popular taverns. The start and final destination were invariably from and to a well-known hostelry. The issue of the New York *Weekly Gazette and Post Boy* for October 1, 1753, contained an announcement that there was a revival of the Burlington stage and wagon. It read:

> Notice is hereby given to all Persons who are inclinable to transport themselves, Goods, Wares, and Merchantdize, from the City of New York to the City of Philadelphia, that they may have the Opportunity of obliging themselves that Way, twice a Week, Wind and Weather permitting.; Daniel O'Bryant, with a commodious Stage Boat, well fitted for that Purpose, will attend at the White Hall Slip, near the Half Moon Battery, at the House of Scots Johnny, in New

Stagecoach from old Mt. Bethel Stage Lines dates from about 1840.

York, in order to receive Goods and Passengers, on Saturday and Wednesday; and on Mondays and Thursdays will set out, and proceed with them to Perth Amboy Ferry, where there is kept a good Stage-Waggon ready to receive them, who on Tuesday and Friday Mornings, set out with them and proceed to the House of John Predmore in Cranbury, where there is kept a fresh Set of Horses and Driver, who immediately proceeds with them the same Day, to the House of Johnathan Thomas in Burlington, where there is kept a commodious Stage-Boat waiting for their reception, Patrick Cowan, Master, who immediately sets out and proceeds with them to the City of Philadelphia.

John Predmore
Daniel O'Brian

Occasionally the signboards outside Jersey taverns had lines that rhymed, such as the following outside a Camden tavern of colonial times:

> I, William Cooper, lives here
> I sell good Ale, Port & Beere,
> I've made my sign a little wider
> To let you know I sell good Cyder.

The verse is noted by an Englishman named Palmer, who visited the United States in 1818 and tells of going over the Jersey countryside from New York to Philadelphia. In his diary, a copy of which is in the New York Historical Society, he says:

We observed several curious tavern signs in Philadelphia and on the Jersey roadside, among others Noah's Ark; a variety of Apostles; Bunyan's Pilgrim; a cock on a lion's back, crowing, with Liberty issuing from his beak; naval engagements in which the British are in a desperate situation; the most common signs are eagles, heads of public figures, Indian Kings, etc.

On occasion the tavern signs along Jersey roadsides are said to have been framed in mourning for the death of a famed public figure, such as Washington or Franklin. At other times they were decorated to mark festive events, such as the Fourth of July.

Bibliography

Boyer, Charles S. *Old Inns & Taverns in West Jersey*. Camden County Historical Society, 1962.

Cawley, James and Margaret. *Along the Old York Road*. New Brunswick, N.J.; Rutgers University Press, 1965.

Chambers, T. F. *The Early Germans in New Jersey*. New York: Dover Press, 1895.

Chastellux, François Jean, Marquis de. *Travels in North America.* Translated by G. Grieve. London, 1787.

Clement, John. *A Sketch of the Life and Character of John Fenwick.* Philadelphia: American Book Co., 1875.

Cunningham, John T. *The Story of Newark.* New Jersey Historical Society, 1964. *The Story of Chatham.* Chatham Historical Society, 1965.

Earle, Alice Morse. *Stage Coach and Tavern Days*. Macmillian Company, 1902. *Home Life in Colonial Days*. Macmillian Company, 1899.

Esdall, Benjamin B. *Address at the First Sussex Contennial Celebration*. 1853. Now out of print.

Glenny, Walter L. *Historic Roadsides of New Jersey*. Society of Colonial Wars, 1928.

Gordon, Thomas F. *A Gazetteer of the State of New Jersey.* Now out of print.

Hageman, John F. *History of Princeton and Its Institutions,* 1879. 2 vols. Now out of print.

Hall, J. F. *History of Atlantic City and County. Atlantic City Daily Union,* 1900.

Hewitt, Louise, *Historic Trenton,* Trenton Public Library, 1916.

Hines, C. G. *The Old Mine Road.* 1909. Distributed by the author. Now out of print.

Hoffman, Robert V. *The Revolutionary Scene in New Jersey.* New York, 1942.

Honeyman, A. Van Doren. *Two Hundred and Fifty Years in Somerset,* 1910. Distributed by the author. Now out of print.

Jones, E. Alfred, *The Loyalists of New Jersey.* New Jersey Historical Society, 1927.

Mellick, Andrew D., Jr. "Story of an Old Farm." Somerville: *The Unionist-Gazette,* 1889.

Podmore, Harry J. *History of Old and New Trenton.* Trenton Public Library, 1927.

Richards, Samuel H. *Early Settlers on or Near the Raccoon.* 1925. Distributed by the author. Now out of print.

Robacker, Earl F. *Touch of the Dutchland.* South Brunswick and New York, A. S. Barnes and Company, 1965.

Salter, Edwin. *A History of Monmouth and Ocean Counties.* Bayonne, N.J., 1890.

Snell, Thomas P. *History of Hunterdon and Somerset Counties. Somerville Messenger,* 1880.

Stockton, Frank P. *Stories of New Jersey.* Philadelphia: American Book Company, 1896.

Thackenthal, B. F. *Improving Navigation on the Delaware River.* Bucks County Historical Society, 1932.

Van Winkle, Daniel. *Old Bergen.* Bayonne, N.J., 1890.

Ward, Christopher. *The Dutch & Swedes on the Delaware, 1609-1664.* Philadelphia, 1930.

Whitehead, W. A. *East Jersey Under the Proprietary Governments, 1875.* Newark, 1875.

BIBLIOGRAPHICAL NOTE: In addition to reading the above, I have visited the offices of the county clerks of the various counties to examine the old license applications, as well as the office of the Secretary of State in Trenton to inspect minutes of the Provincial Congress and the New Jersey Council of Safety. I have also visited and spent many hours in the New Jersey Historical Society in Newark, the Rutgers University Library in New Brunswick, The New Jersey Society,

Sons of the American Revolution, now in Elizabeth and formerly in Newark, as well as the New York Historical Society and the Holland Society of New York, both in New York City, and various public libraries in cities around the state to inspect and read old diaries, maps, correspondence, and books not in my own library.

Index

Adams, John, 30, 147
Adams, Samuel, 46
Alden, John, 138
Alexander, Philip, 87
Allaire, James P., 137
Alloway Tavern, 85
Allen House, 137
Allen Tavern, 129
Allen, William, 82
American Hotel, 137
American House, 135
Anderson, Carl K., 144
Anderson, John, 42, 52, 53, 133, 139
Applegate, George, 78, 135
Archer, Joseph, 80
Arney, Joseph, 81
Arneytown, 81
Arnold, Col. Jacob, 35
Arnold, Samuel, 34
Arnold Tavern, 34
Aspden, Mathias, 93
Asylum, Elizabeth, 51
Atchley, Jesse, 123
Atkinson, Philip, 68
Atkinson, Thomas, 79, 80
Aumock, Andrew, 46
Axford, Charles, 132

Bagley, William, 74
Bainridge, 77
Baker, Samuel, 87
Ball, Marcus, 38
Barber, Samuel, 87
Barber's Tavern, 89
Barlow, Joel, 170

Barnhill, John, 6, 127
Barns, John, 137
Baskington Ridge, 36
Basnett, Richard, 74
Basnett Tavern, 74
Bayton, Peter, 76
Bear Tavern, 122
Bedminster, 45, 106
Bedminster Inn, 106
Beekman, Christopher, 129
Beekman Tavern, 130
Belcher, Jonathan, 51
Bellin, Mrs. Ellis, 38
Bergen, Jacob G., 59
Bergen (Jersey City), 44
Berger, Casper, 45
Berrian Mansion, 129
Bethlehem, 121
Biddle Tavern, 86
Biddle, William, 86
Bishop, Joseph, 136
Bishop Tavern, 136
Bispham's Tavern, 148
Black Horse Tavern, 36, 37, 131
Black Sam's Tavern, 44, 45
Blair, Peter, 107
Blazing Star Tavern, 134
Blimm, 116
Bloomfield, Govenor, 166
Blue Anchor, 145
Blue Anchor Tavern, 75, 76
Blue Hills Plantation, 167
Blue Hills Tavern, 94
Boars Head Tavern, 121
Bolton, Isaac, 96

Bonnel, Abraham, 40, 121
Bonnel's, Tavern, 40
Borden, Joseph, 77, 78
Bordentown, 77, 135
Boucher, James, 94
Boudinot, Elias, 51
Boudinot Hall, 100
Bound Brook, 66
Boyer, Charles S., 84, 136
Brewster's Tavern, 105
Brick House, 99
Brick House Tavern, 61, 79, 32
Bridgeboro, 82
Bridgeport, 94
Bridgeton, 94
Bridgewater, 36
Brierley, John, 89
Britton, Charity, 61, 132
Britton, Issac, 132
Brown, Dr. Joseph, 78, 135
Brown, Mark, 139
Brown's Tavern, 78
Bullion's Tavern, 105
Burlington, 25, 72
Burr, John Jr., 79
Burrough, Edward, 89
Butcher, John Jr., 77
Buter, John Sr., 80
Byram, 69
Byram, Alpheus, 61
Byram, Ebenezer, 36

Calvin, Luther, 69
Camden, 90
Campbell, George, 59
Cannonball House, 112, 153
Cape May City, 95
Carman, Joshua, 135
Carteret Arms, 51, 101
Carteret, Philip, 17
Carter, Spencer, 42, 121
Centerton Tavern, 86
Centerville, 67
Champney, Joseph, 87
Chatham, 42
Chattin, Abraham, 97
City Hotel, 130, 134
Clark, Elisha, 146
Clark, Roger, 31, 99
Clayton, John, 78
Clinton, 38, 121

Clinton, De Witt, 38
Clinton House, 38, 39
Clunn, Joseph, 61, 131
Coats, John, 68
Cock & Bull, 106
Coddington, Louis, 158
Codrington, Thomas, 66
Coffin, William, 96
Colligan, Charles, 123
Colonial American Hotel, 55, 128
Columbus, 80
Congleton, Allen, 87
Connel, John, 68
Cooper, Benjamin, 91
Cooper, Daniel, 91
Cooper, James B. 133
Cooper, James B., 133
Cooper, Samuel, 91
Cooper's Point, 91
Cooper's Tavern, 91
Cooperstown Tavern, 83
Cornell House, 65
Coryll, George, 126
Cotting, Elias, 95
Counties, 73
Cowenhoven, Daniel, 120
Cox, Richards, 80
Crabb, William, 85
Craig, William, 87
Cranbury, 140
Cranbury Inn, 140
Craven, Richard, 85
Crawford, Archbald, 87
Crawford, John, 40
Crawford's Corner, 40
Crawford Tavern, 41
Creed, Dr. James, 42
Creighton, Hugh, 92
Crooked Billet Tavern, 80
Cross and Key, 127
Cross Keys Inn, 79
Crosswicks, 77

D'Agostino, M. J. (Doc), 140
Darby, John, 82
Daretown, 86
Daretown Tavern, 86
Davis, John, 147
Day, Isreal, 43
Day's Tavern, 43
Day, Timothy, 42, 43

Dayton, Charles, 86
Death of the Fox Tavern, 93
Dennis, John, 50
De Witt, Henry, 30
Dewitt, Simson, 166
Dickerson Tavern, 104
Dickinson, John, 85
Donaldson, Arthur, 92
Doughtery, Edmond, 87
Douglas, Thomas, 77
Drake, Mrs. Isabell, 46
Drinker, Elizabeth, 58
Duffill, Peter, 86
Duke de la Rochefoucault, 147
Dunham, John, 139

Eagle Tavern, 43, 101, 102
Eaton, Harriet Phillips, 44
Edsall, James, 76
Eldridge, Reuben, 83
Elizabeth, 49, 100
Elizabethtown, 16, 49, 51, 101
Elwell, Jacob, 86
Emley, John, 42
Englishtown, 62, 142
Erskine, Gen. Robert, 34, 166
Evans, Caleb, 81

Farmer's Hotel, 116
Farnesworth, 42
Fenimore, David, 135
Fields Tavern, 62
Finigan, Christian, 75
Fish, Benjamin, 132
Fisher, Jeremiah, 46
Fisher Tavern, 66, 117
Flatbrookville, 32, 99
Fleming, Samuel, 42, 69
Flourish, Arthur, 117
Fopp, Outhout, 84
Follet, George, 130
Fox, George, 163, 164
Franklin, Benjamin, 147
Freas, Jacob, 86
Freehold, 137
Frenchtown, 69
Fulkerson, William, 107

Gates, Horatio, 30
Gaunt, Joseph, 80
Gerrard, Robert, 94
Gibbs, Isaac, 80
Gifford, Amos, 102

Gifford, Archer, 46
Gifford, John, 130
Gifford's Tavern, 102
Gloeckner's Tavern, 117
Gloucester Town, 89
Godfrey, Benjamin, 95
Goodwin, David, 130
Graham's Tavern, 51
Grant, Robert, 68
Grant, Ulysses S., 48
Graves, Samuel, 89
Greeley, Horace, 48
Green Tree Inn, 133
Griffen, William, 84
Grover, William H., 82
Grubb, Henry, 76, 149
Guttridge's Tavern, 115

Hackensack, 33
Hackettstown, 37
Haddonfield, 92
Haight, Joseph, 76
Halfway House, 113
Hall, Abigail, 78
Hall, John, 95
Hall, Lodowick, 88
Hall's Tavern, 95
Hall, William, 84
Halsey's Tavern, 103
Hancock's Bridge, 87
Harris, Abel, 88
Hart, Jack, 38
Hart, John, 123
Hay, Thomas, 78
Haynes, Benjamin, 85
Heath, Samuel, 46
Henderson, Thomas, 121
Herbert, Daniel, 142
Hewarie, Arthur, 46
Hickory Tavern, 41, 42, 121
Hicks, William, 57
Hier, Jacob, 60
Hillman, John, 91
Hillman, Joseph, 139
Hillman, Josiah, 139
Hines, C. G., 30, 162
Historic Inn, 153
Hoagland's Tavern, 135
Hoagland, Oakes, 134, 135
Hogan, Oakley, 135
Hollingham, Isaac, 89
Hollingshead, John, 74
Hollingshead, Joseph, 76

Hopper, Lettes, 62
Horner, John, 80
Horner, Samuel, 57
Horse Neck, 33, 34
Hotel Waldorf, 117
Hounds and Horn Tavern, 102, 146
Howard, William, 107
Howell, Benjamin, 94
Howell, Daniel, 68
Howell, John, 133
Howell, Peter, 42, 121
Howell's Ferry, 68
Hudibras, 57
Hugg, Joseph, 90, 139
Hugg's Tavern, 90
Hulme, George, 75
Hunlock, Thomas, 74
Hunt, Daniel, 39
Hunt's Mills 38, 40
Hutchinson, John, 83
Hyer, Jacob, 130

Indian King Tavern, 132
Indian Queen Tavern, 55, 100, 128, 133
Insloe, Peter, 87

Jacob Gibb's Inn, 96
James B. Cooper's Inn, 133
Jefkin, Dudwick, 107
Jegou, Peter, 72
Jersey City, 44
Jobstown, 83
Jockey Hollow Road, 35
Johnson, Asher, 123
Johnson, Jacob Jr., 122
Johnson, John, 62
Johnson, Thomas, 16
Joline, John, 130
Jones, Capt. Thomas, 41
Jones, Daniel, 79
Jones, John, 85, 92
Jones, Stephen, 90
Jones Tavern, 122
Jones, Thomas, 122
Joseph Burrough's Tavern, 86

Kaighn, Joseph, 92
Kaighn's Point, 92
Kay, Samuel, 133
Keen, Mounce, 86
Keen's Tavern, 95
Kenilworth Inn, 129

Ketchum, Theopolis, 67
King George Inn, 70, 172
King of Prussia Tavern, 132
King's Arms Tavern, 58, 60, 131, 171, 172
King's Highway, 49, 51, 52, 53
Kinney, Thomas, 35
Kitts, Robert, 87

Laconey, Samuel, 82
Lafayette, Marquis de, 147, 148
Laing's Hotel, 116
Lambert, John, 125
Lambertville, 68, 125, 127
Lambertville House, 125
Lambson, Hance, 88
Lambson House, 88
Lambson, Mathias, 88
Lamington Falls, 45
Larison's Corner, 119
Larison's Tavern, 119
Lawrie House, 81
Lawrie, William, 81
Liberty Corner, 45
Ligonier Tavern, 62
Lindsay, William, 94
Lippencott, Job Jr., 83
Livingston, William, 11
Lloyd, John, 89
Lloyd, Obadiah, 88, 89
Lloyd, Solomon, 88
Long Ferry Tavern, 55, 56
Louderbach, Peter, 88
Lovelace, Governor, 18
Lovett, Aaron, 77
Lowery, Nathaniel, 42, 123
Ludlum, Jacob Jr., 96
Lukas, Aaron T., 41, 46, 120
Lyon, Henry, 16
Lyon's Farm, 16

McElroy, Archibald, 76
Mackay Tavern, 122
Marshall, James, 125
Marsh, John, 112
Matlock, John, 122
Medcalfe, Mathew, 89
Mellick, Andrew Jr., 157
Mellick, John, 106
Mendham, 33, 36
Mercereau, John, 52, 127, 160, 161
Merchant's and Drover Tavern, 52, 127, 160

Mershon, Andrew, 123
Mestayer, Daniel, 85
Meyer, Henry C., 112
Montague, 31, 99
Moon, James, 77
Morford, Zebulon, 130
Morris Ave., 42, 43
Morris, John, 50
Morris, Robert H., 69
Morristown, 34, 36, 104
Mount Bethel, 70
Mountere, 57
Mount Holly, 79
Mount Pleasant, 138
Mount Pleasant Tavern, 138
Muir, Alexander, 112
Mulford, Daniel, 136
Mulliner, Joseph, 96
Murdock, William, 85

Nassau Inn, 50, 130
Native American Tavern, 133
Nelson, Abraham, 88
Nesco, 96
Newark 43, 101
New Brunswick, 55, 128
New England, 15
New Germantown, 46
New Hampton, 122
New Jersey Assembly, 17
New Jersey Dragon Tavern, 134
Newton, 33
New White House, 120
New York, 28
Nicholls, Governor, 17
Norris, Robert, 104
Norris, Sarah, 92
Norris, Thomas, 89

Odgen, John, 79
O'Hanlon, Patrick, 76
Old Mill, 63
Old Mine Road, 28, 33, 129
Old Stage House Inn, 64
Oldwick, 46
Old York Road, 100, 111
Orange, South, 37
Ordinaries, 148
Osborne, Johnathon, 113
Osborne's Tavern, 113
Outhout Tavern, 84
Oxford, 37
Oxford Furnace, 30, 37

Packer House, 134
Pahaquarry, 29, 32
Palles Hook, 58
Parker, Nathaniel, 42, 123
Parvin, Silas, 95
Passaic, 34
Passaic River, 15
Paullin, Jacobs, 88
Peapack-Gladstone, 45
Penn's Charter, 34
Pennsville, 87
Penton, Abner, 85
Perth Amboy, 55, 134
Peters, Benjamin, 94
Peter Zabriskie House, 33
Philadelphia, 33
Pine Tavern, 94
Plainfield, 115, 116
Platt, Richard, 81
Poets Inn, 138
Polhemus, John, 132
Port Jervis, 33
Potter, Mathew Jr., 136
Potters Mills, 45
Potters Tavern, 136
Pottersville, 45, 108
Pottersville Hotel, 46, 108
Potts, Richard, 81
Powell, John, 68
Predmore, John, 75, 140
Pregmore, Daniel, 69
Price, Robert, 92
Princeton, 56, 129
Princeton University, 55, 57
Probasco, Peter, 133
Pulaski, Casimir, 30
Pumpkin Tavern, 87

Rain, Timothy, 94
Raritan, 65
Raritan River, 39, 40
Reading, John, 68
Readington, 67
Red Lion Inn, 50, 51, 100, 172
Rice, Thomas, 85
Richards, John, 78
Richards, Joseph, 83
Ridley, James, 84
Ringoes, 67, 119
Ringo, John, 68
Ringo, Philip, 67
Ringwood, 34
Rising Sun Tavern, 43, 80, 103

Roberts, Jesse, 120
Robeson, Joseph, 68
Rockefeller, Peter John, 119
Rockhill, Solomon, 80
Rocky Hill, 128
Roff, Moses, 103
Roselle, 51
Rose, Philip, 46
Rossell, Zachariah 79
Ross, John, 90
Royal Oak, 62
Royal Oaks, 131
Royden, William, 52, 91
Runyan, Samuel H., 139
Rutherford, Robert, 62
Ryland Inn, 70

Sailor Bay Hotel, 96
St. George Ave., 53
Salem Town, 83, 84
Samuel Fleming Tavern, 123
Scotch Plains, 64, 111
Scudder, Abner, 133
Scudder, Benjamin, 155
Scull, Samuel, 145
Scull Tavern, 145
Sculltown Tavern, 87
Seabury's Inn, 103
Shaw, John, 76
Sherron's Tavern, 85
Ship and Castle Tavern, 13, 131
Shoemaker, Henry, 30, 31
Shreve, Thomas, 75
Shrewsbury, 137
Sibley, John, 137
Sign of the Angel Tavern, The, 75
Sign of the College, 58
Sign of the Fox Tavern, 134
Sign of the Gen. Wolfe, 76
Sign of the Hudibras, 59, 60, 130
Sign of the Punch Bowl, 78
Skillman, Abraham, 162
Somerville, 118
Somerville Hotel, 118
Souder, Simon, 136
Sourland Mountain, 47
South Orange Hotel, 37
Sparks, John, 88
Sparks, Henry, 91
Sparks, Randall, 139
Sparks, Richard, 86
Sparks, Thomas, 75
Squire, F. C., 52, 53

Squire, Harriet, 53
Stanbury, Jacob, 112
Stanbury, Recompense, 26, 111
Staples, Thomas, 75
Steib, B. J., 164
Stewart, Charles, 121
Stille, Rachel, 62, 131
Still, Pontius, 133
Still's Tavern, 133
Stockton, 68
Stockton Inn, 123, 125
Stockton, Richard, 58
Stoll, Judge James, 32
Stretch, James, 87
Sutton's Hotel, 46
Swan, Amos, 113, 114
Swan's Tavern, 113
Swesey, Amos, 122
Swedesboro, 87
Swift Sure Stage Line, 157, 158

Tatem, John, 91
Tatem, William, 91
Tavern in the Woods, 47
Taylor, Christopher, 93
Taylor, Robert, 139
Teeple, Henry, 46
Ten Eyck, Jacob, 130
Thomas, Edward, 50
Thomas, Jonathon, 76
Thomas, Robinson, 50
Thompson, Col. Mark, 121
Thompson, John, 43, 130, 161
Thompson, Joseph, 85
Thompson, Samuel, 38
Thorn, John, 78
Three Run Tavern, 79
Tise's Tavern, 44
Tonkins, Isreal, 77
Tours House, 44
Treadway, Henry, 89
Trenton, 60, 131
Tucker, Reuben, 80
Tuckerton, 80
Tunison, Cornelius, 120
Tunison's Tavern, 66
Turkey (New Providence), 43
Twining, Thomas, 146

Union Hotel, 31, 50, 81, 137, 157
Union Tavern, 91, 132, 139
United States Hotel, 133

Van Campen, Abraham, 30
Van Campen House, 99
Van Campen Inn, 30
Van Horn, Abraham, 41, 120
Van Horn, Arthur, 41
Van Horn, Cornelius, 120
Van Ripen, Daniel, 45
Van Syckle, Peter, 121
Vermeule, Cornelius, 167
Village House, 63
Village Inn, 143

Wallace House, 118
Walpack Township, 30, 31, 99
Walpole's Hotel, 114
Wansey, Henry, 146
Ward, Matthias, 43, 161
Ware, Joel, 83
Warford, Aaron, 69
Warford Tavern, 69
Washington House, 77, 91, 109
Washington Inn, 129
Watchung, 45, 109
Wayne, Gen. Anthony, 45
Webb, George, 89
Webb, Perry, 92
Welsh, John, 46
Welter, Conrad, 32
Wescott, Col. Richard, 146
West, Benjamin, 149
Westcott's Tavern, 146
West Point, 45
Wheat Sheaf Inn, 51, 52, 127
Whitehead Tavern, 128
Whitehead, William, 59

White House, 41, 120
White House Tavern, 120
Wiggins, James, 85
Wilkenson, Peter, 83
Wilkinson, John, 83
Wilkins, Thomas, 94
Williamson, Mathias, 50
Williamson, William, 50
Windham, Henry, 117
Windsor Chair, 26
Windsor, George, 79
Wistarburg Tavern, 88
Wistar, Casper, 86
Woodbury, 90
Wood, James, 91
Wood, Jehu, 91
Wood, Samuel, 139
Woods Tavern, 47
Woodstown, 88
Wrangel, Rev. Carl, 144
Wright, Fretwell, 75
Wright, John, 83
Wrightstown, 83
Wrightstown Tavern, 83
Wycoff, John, 46

Yard, Isaiah, 131
Yard, John, 131
Yard, Joseph, 59
Yard's Inn, 61
Yard Tavern, 131
Yard, William, 60
York, Duke of, 18
York Road, 64